"A Kind of Alaska"

Women in the Plays of
O'Neill, Pinter, and Shepard

Ann C. Hall

Southern Illinois University Press / *Carbondale and Edwardsville*

Library of Congress Cataloging-in-Publication Data

Hall, Ann C., 1959–
    "A kind of Alaska" : women in the plays of O'Neill, Pinter,
and Shepard / Ann C. Hall.
        p.   cm.
    Includes bibliographical references and index.
    1. American drama—20th century—History and criticism.
    2. Women in literature. 3. O'Neill, Eugene, 1888–1953—
    Characters—Women. 4. Pinter, Harold, 1930–   —Char-
    acters—Women 5. Shepard, Sam, 1943–   —Characters—
    Women.   I. Title.
    PS338.W6H34   1993
    812′.509352042—dc20   92-35621
    ISBN 0-8093-1877-6   CIP

The paper used in this publication meets the minimum
requirements of American National Standard for Information
Sciences—Permanence of Paper for Printed Library Materials,
ANSI Z39.48-1984. ∞

For my family,
particularly the memory of
Louis P. Molnar

Contents

Acknowledgments

THROUGHOUT the preparation of this book, I have been very fortunate to have met so many helpful colleagues, teachers, and friends. I would first like to thank Katherine Burkman for all her suggestions during this book's early drafts. She is a wonderful teacher, scholar, and friend. To my colleague at Marquette University, Michael Gillespie, I offer my sincerest thanks for reading sections of this manuscript and offering sound and humorous advice. Thanks, too, to my graduate students in modern drama, particularly Joan Navarre. To Yuan Zhang, my research assistant, I extend my gratitude for her patience and persistence. I am grateful to Marquette University for the two grants that gave me the time to revise and rethink this project. I am especially thankful for Judith Roof, Carolyn Asp, and Grace Epstein. Their insightful discussions regarding feminist and Lacanian theory were invaluable. Gail Finney's suggestions regarding a later revision of this manuscript were extremely helpful. Thanks, too, to Carol Burns and Curtis Clark of Southern Illinois University Press. The Contemporary American Theatre Company not only provided me with a leave of absence in order to complete this project but also taught and continues to teach me new ways of seeing theatre. Finally, I would like to thank Geoff Nelson without whose support and sense of humor this project would not have been complete.

"A Kind of Alaska"

1

Introduction

The road is covered in snow and, inside the coach, the somber lady wrapped in furs feels bored. Suddenly she calls out the name of one of the girls in her train. The girl is brought to her: the Countess bites her frantically and sticks needles in her flesh. A while later the procession abandons the wounded girl in the snow. The girl tries to run away. She is pursued, captured and pulled back into the coach. A little further along the road they halt: the Countess has ordered cold water. Now the girl is naked, standing in the snow. Night has fallen. A circle of torches surrounds her, held out by impassive footmen. They pour water over her body and the water turns to ice. (The Countess observes this from the coach.) The girl attempts one last slight gesture, trying to move closer to the torches — the only source of warmth. More water is poured over her, and there she remains, for ever standing, upright, dead.
    —Alejandra Pizarnik, "The Bloody Countess"

I account this world a tedious theatre,
For I do play a part in't against my will.
    —John Webster, *The Duchess of Malfi*

Turning to the French is a form of suicide for the American who loves literature — or, as the joke might go, it is at least a cry for help.
    —Annie Dillard, *An American Childhood*

THIS book offers a feminist, psychoanalytic reading of the plays of Eugene O'Neill, Harold Pinter, and Sam Shepard. In it, I argue that the female characters are not only significant to the dramas in which they appear, but that more importantly, through these female characters, the plays expose the process by which patriarchy attempts to oppress women. In many instances, moreover, the female characters resist such oppression and eventually encourage their audiences and their fictional male counterparts to reconsider female oppression. While this project does not entirely defend these male authors' representations of women, my study does encourage and argue for a greater appreciation of their female characters through a feminist, psychoanalytic approach. Given the spirited debates concerning feminism, feminist readings, and psychoanalytic approaches occurring within the academic profession and outside it, such claims demand elaboration.

First, and simply put, feminism focuses on analyzing, examining, and changing the oppressed status of women and the oppressive modes of representing women throughout culture. Such a broad definition affords much room for interpretation and discussion, which is precisely what is occurring in feminist studies today. In terms of the dramatic and literary tradition, a tradition that has overlooked and dismissed the important contributions of women to the field, feminist critics have focused their energies on bringing the contributions of female playwrights, performers, directors, critics, and theatre companies to light.[1] Unlike scholarly, feminist studies of the novel that began by examining the representation of women in male-authored texts, modern feminist dramatic criticism is characterized by its focus on women's work and its argument for such work's validity and marketability. The economic realities of theatrical productions play a big part in creating this trend. Producers are reluctant to support any unknown or controversial work in their attempts to sustain and increase ticket sales. Clearly, promoting work by women in theatre is an important and necessary component of feminist criticism.

Another factor behind this female focus in dramatic criticism is less pragmatic. As Rita Felski notes, the work of feminist literary critics, particularly Americans, is often characterized by the assumption that male authors cannot create "real" female characters (26). The following question by Hélène Cixous, a question that shaped this book, not only articulates the problematic relationship between the female spectator and traditional, male-authored dramas, but it is also one of the most arresting examples of this line of reasoning. I realize, of course, that Cixous is French, but as Felski makes clear, the assumption that defines feminist American literary criticism often includes non-Americans (20). Cixous asks,

> How, as women, can we go to the theatre without lending our complicity to the sadism directed against women, or being asked to assume, in the patriarchal family structure that the theatre reproduces *ad infinitum*, the position of victim? ("Aller" 546)

According to Cixous, traditional, male-authored dramas require that female spectators not only have no one to identify with, but these dramas, in fact, require that female spectators position themselves in the role of the sadistic countess of Alejandra Pizarnik's narrative, a story that illustrates a woman victimizing another woman. For Cixous, as for many other feminists, the appropriate and perhaps the only feminist solution to such a situation is to focus on women's contributions.

While most feminist critics of modern drama do not state this assumption or view as clearly as Cixous, the limited number of feminist studies on modern dramatic texts by male authors may indicate that such studies are not considered an important activity for feminist scholars. Those few studies that have appeared—particularly on the female characters in O'Neill, Pinter, and Shepard—are haunted by this assumption. These studies presume that a feminist text must include a "real" and oftentimes triumphant or entirely sympathetic female character.[2] Felski, who calls such approaches *gynocritical*, notes that these readings presume that patriarchy is a "homogeneous and uniformly regressive phenomenon" (26–27). Of greater importance to the feminist critic, however, is the presumption that feminism or feminist readings are also homogeneous.

And here is where the problem arises. Focusing on female contributions is important, but it becomes problematic when it becomes the sole characteristic of feminist readings. Feminist theorist Annette Kolodny offers a broader definition of a feminist reading that avoids such assumptions but that does not compromise feminist concerns:

> All the feminist is asserting, then, is her own equivalent right to liberate new (and perhaps different) significances from these same texts; and at the same time, her right to choose which features of the text she takes as relevant because she is, after all, asking new and different questions of it. In the process, she claims neither definitiveness nor structural completeness for her different readings and reading systems, but only their usefulness in recognizing the particular achievements of woman-as-author and their applicability in conscientiously decoding woman-as-sign. ("Dancing" 160)

Kolodny's definition clearly avoids the oppressive role of the female spectator. It does not mimic the oppression of the patriarchy it is attempting to challenge and change. According to Kolodny, the feminist literary critic seeks to discuss the text but not impose meaning upon the work. This does not imply that "anything goes," but Kolodny, like many poststructuralist critics, seeks to explore and take into account the play of signification exhibited by literary texts rather than enforcing either a rigid definition of feminism or aesthetics. Such limited definitions ignore the dynamic nature of art, as well as feminism, a dynamism that is illustrated both in the academic profession and popular culture. One only has to turn to the "Oprah" television show, Cable News Network (CNN), or the *Publications of the Modern Language Association* for examples. Kolodny argues for a pluralistic interpretation of feminism and literary criticism, one that embraces, according to Rita Felski, "differing and often conflicting positions" (13). Focusing on the female characters in male-authored texts, then, is not only valid but a necessary feminist and dramatic task.

Shakespeare scholarship has been especially graced with compelling studies of female characters from a feminist perspective.[3] And such studies are beginning to appear in the field of modern drama as well, perhaps marking a new trend in feminist dramatic criticism. Gail Finney's *Women in Modern Drama*, for example, avoids the reductive feminist method and assumption by focusing on the processes of the Freudian theory, but she does not address the problem of female representation by male authors in the late modern and contemporary theatre. June Schlueter's collection *Feminist Rereadings of Modern American Drama* and Linda Ben-Zvi's *Women in Beckett* offer sterling examples of feminist examinations of women in modern dramatic texts by male authors. Few full-length studies are available, however, and none employ the psychoanalytic technique I intend to use. The purpose of this study, then, is to approach the texts of Eugene O'Neill, Harold Pinter, and Sam Shepard from a feminist perspective that reduces neither the complexities of the dramatic texts nor feminism.

Many factors led me to this project, to my choice of these three modern authors, and especially to my use of psychoanalytic theory. What I hope to avoid throughout the book is a slavish adherence to the precepts of psychoanalytic theory when approaching these texts. Instead, I hope to borrow relevant concepts that offer some explanation for the problematic representation of women in the plays of O'Neill, Pinter, and Shepard.

I chose these particular playwrights for several reasons. All three authors are immensely popular and important to the modern dramatic tradition, and all three underwent a period of experimentation during their early years as writers. In their later works, which many consider the height of their creative powers, they employed realistic conventions. Of particular importance, all three used the domestic setting for these later dramas. For a feminist, this setting is noteworthy because the home and the family have been the centers of female oppression both on stage and off. Furthermore, the female characters in these dramas are decidedly problematic. In many plays, women are not even physically present, but the male characters continue to discuss, remember, and manipulate offstage female characters to such an extent that the presence of women becomes a major factor in such plays, despite their absence. In those dramas that do contain onstage female characters, something is always missing. They are emotionally or mentally absent. Like Webster's Duchess of Malfi, they apparently are forced to play a part against their will. Many critical explanations for this mode of female representation reflect the general tendency of American criticism, as discussed by Felski: male authors could only create Madonnas or whores, the extreme and mutually exclusive categories available to women within a patriarchal culture. While such criticism is often true of these and other male dramatists, it became the predominant mode critics used in approaching the female characters in the plays of O'Neill, Pinter, and Shepard. The female characters were characterized as nothing more than stage property, props to uphold the male performance and spectacle. Oftentimes, the authors were condemned for such representations because they were not "real" enough. As Rita Felski notes, feminist criticism that expects "real" representations of women does not take the question of female subjectivity into account (51). And while Felski does not entirely approve of the work of feminist, psychoanalytic theory, such theories constitute much of the recent discussion of female subjectivity.

Admittedly, the relationship between psychoanalysis and feminism has been uneasy. In one of the earliest discussions of the two, Juliet Mitchell's *Psychoanalysis and Feminism*, Freud's participation in female oppression is questioned: was he highlighting the misogynistic, cultural models of the age or legitimizing them? With the appearance of Freud's revisionist, psychoanalytic theorist Jacques Lacan, the question remained but the debate heightened. In her extremely helpful and readable book, *Jacques Lacan: A Feminist Introduction*, Elizabeth Grosz notes:

Lacan continues to be one of the most controversial figures within contemporary feminist theory. Many feminists use his work on human subjectivity to challenge phallocentric knowledges; others are extremely hostile to it, seeing it as elitist, male-dominated, and itself phallocentric. (147)

Of particular concern to this study is the question of female identity, but on this point, too, much of the disagreement between feminism and psychoanalysis occurs. For both Freud and Lacan, the female subject is different from the male, but as history has demonstrated and as Felski emphasizes, this difference is often the means by which patriarchy justifies its oppression of women. Because the debates are so spirited, the problems that many feminist and nonfeminist literary critics have with psychoanalytic theory requires discussion, a discussion that can begin with the question of female difference.

What the attacks against female difference ignore is the Freudian context of Lacan's remarks. According to Freud, women are castrated, lacking the penis. Men, however, possess the penis, and are afforded a great deal of power as a result. What Lacan implies and what I find so revolutionary about his theory is that he demonstrates that all human subjects "lack." Male subjects do not have anything more than women. As a matter of fact, Lacan implies that women have a better understanding of the human condition and therefore a better understanding of existence and a greater opportunity for self-knowledge. Admittedly, such an argument is problematic for a feminist who has been struggling against male definitions of femininity in order to define her own feminine identity. But Lacan stresses that definitions of gender are constructed by the patriarchy's desire to create an imaginary sense of psychic completion. Thus, Lacan offers an explanation and an illustration of the invisibility of women within the patriarchal system.

According to Lacan, all human subjects are constituted by lack: something is always missing. The human condition for Lacan, however, is characterized by a continual misreading, a *méconnaissance*, which presumes and assumes an autonomous identity. The crucial point for Lacan is the *mirror* stage, his addition to the Freudian stages of development. Prior to the mirror stage, the Lacanian subject experiences unadulterated unity with the mother. With the mirror stage, a precursor to the oedipal conflict, however, the subject perceives his separateness from the mother. In Lacan's words, it is

> a drama whose internal thrust is precipitated from insufficiency to anticipation—and which manufactures for the subject, caught up in the lure of spatial identification, the succession of phantasies that extends from a fragmented body-image to a form of its totality that I shall call orthopaedic—and, lastly, to the assumption of the armour of an alienating identity, which will mark with its rigid structure the subject's entire mental development. (*Ecrits* 4)

At this moment, which actually occurs for the subject at eighteen months of age but is reproduced figuratively throughout his life, the subject leaves the pre-oedipal state of unity with the mother and discovers his individuality through the mirror image. The reflected image presents an autonomous body-image that the subject assumes to be his. Simultaneously, however, comes the realization that the image is exterior, thereby diminishing the jubilation of "self-reliance." As Kaja Silverman notes, the subject "loves the coherent identity which the mirror provides." However, she continues, "because the image remains external to it, it also hates that image" (158). Rather than recognizing this inherent paradox of existence, the subject embarks on a quest for the perfect mirror that will reproduce the jubilant sense of autonomy, but without the attendant anxiety.

One of the problems with this moment is that at the time, the subject does not consciously realize the occurrence. Once the subject enters what Lacan calls the *symbolic* stage, the arena of language and culture, the subject experiences lack and remembers the moments during the mirror and the pre-oedipal stages that gave him the sense of complete fulfillment. These memories, which are characteristic of what Lacan calls the *imaginary*, the stage at which the subject perceives himself as whole and complete, continue to haunt the symbolic, the next stage of development; that is, once the subject enters the symbolic, he perceives lack. However, he still desires the sense of autonomy that he experienced during the jubilant moment of the mirror stage.[4] This desire prompts the subject to search for an "other" that would, paradoxically, recreate the sense of psychic completion for him.

According to Lacan, while women participate in the mirror stage, they do not participate in it as completely as men. Instead, women often serve as the mirror for male desire, what Lacan calls the *petit objet a*, the other that will bring about masculine fulfillment (Lacan, *Feminine Sexuality*, 138–48; Silverman 186). Of course, Lacan is not the first to make this claim. In *A Room of One's Own*, Virginia Woolf claims:

> Women have served all these centuries as looking-glasses possessing the magic and delicious power of reflecting the figure of man at twice its natural size. . . . Whatever may be their use in civilised societies, mirrors are essential to all violent and heroic action. That is why Napoleon and Mussolini both insist so emphatically upon the inferiority of women, for if they were not inferior, they would cease to enlarge. . . . For if she begins to tell the truth, the figure in the looking-glass shrinks. . . . (35–36)

What Lacan emphasizes is that women are forced into this role by men, language, and culture. Female desire is denied, and when a man grows weary of his current female mirror, which he inevitably does, he searches for "other" women rather than examining his own misreading of existence (*Feminine Sexuality* 84–85). Women must merely play a part in this psychic, male drama, a role they often play against their will or desires.

For Lacan, like many postmodern theorists, signification is, if not entirely responsible for this oppression, an important factor in perpetuating female objectification. Like Derrida, Lacan argues that language is based upon a dialectic of power, namely the exclusion of one term in order to create the existence of the other, more powerful term. This is what he defines as the *phallocentric* nature of language. When it comes to sexual difference and its representation, then, masculinity is defined by the exclusion of femininity. Women are objectified, alienated, and defined merely as "not men."[5] According to Lacan, "there is only woman as excluded by the nature of things which is the nature of words" (*Feminine Sexuality* 144). In short, *woman* becomes a construct that upholds the illusion of male autonomy (Rose, *Feminine Sexuality* 137). Consequently, female representation or participation in such a polarized discourse is troublesome at best.

Judith Butler's accusations that Lacan creates a sadistic system of subjectivity are particularly justified when approaching the position of women in this scenario (43–50). For while Lacan recognizes the slippage in the formal objectified system of signification caused by femininity, he also implies that it has little effect, given the omnipresent, phallocentric linguistic system. And here many critics have difficulty with Lacan, for this formulation implies that women in fact do not have access to language and, by association, to political change. For all of Lacan's revolutionary ideology, then, he apparently places women in the position where they have always resided: silent, other, victim. Any feminine discourse, by its very nature, would also be subject to the dialectics of oppression.

The inevitability of this linguistic prison is difficult to ignore in the works of Lacan. As Luce Irigaray, who was once his student, notes,

> Women's social inferiority is reinforced and complicated by the fact that woman does not have access to language, except through recourse to "masculine" systems of representation which disappropriates her from her relation to herself and to other women. (*This Sex* 85)

Irigaray, however, neither accepts this situation as inevitable nor proposes the utopian vision of a separate female language as espoused by proponents of *l'écriture féminine*.[6] Instead, she proposes a change within language: "Rather than maintaining the masculine-feminine opposition, it would be appropriate to seek a possibility of *non-hierarchical* articulation of that difference in language" (*This Sex* 162). As Elizabeth Grosz explains,

> Her assault on patriarchal language consists in showing that those discourses which present themselves as universal and neutral, appropriate to all, are in fact produced and maintained according to male interests. (177)

In this way, Irigaray illustrates that not only is the hierarchical dialectic of male/female a construct, but it is a construct that can be dismantled.

Nowhere is this strategy better demonstrated than in Irigaray's two books that offer subtle but profound methods for thwarting such linguistic and political oppression. In *Speculum of the Other Woman*, for example, she imaginatively positions herself as a feminist interrogator at Freud's problematic lecture on femininity. Through a series of questions, which are based upon psychoanalytic principles, she exposes the gaps and assumptions that the lecture attempts to ignore. By "creating a stir," she throws Freudian theory into question, without resorting to yet another oppressive dialectic of power; that is, she does not merely invert the male-female dialectic, but instead, she articulates feminine difference that threatens the coherence of the Freudian scenario. In *This Sex Which Is Not One*, Irigaray illustrates the connection between the linguistic and the political oppression of women. Defined as "not men," women have functioned as commodities in the sexual, patriarchal marketplace. Their only function has been to insure the perpetuation of the phallic economy. Consequently, any resistance creates anxiety on the sexual stock exchange—when the object, previously presumed mute, speaks, there is trouble.

Irigaray's solution has raised debates among feminist critics. Rita Felski, for example, argues that it merely places women in yet another reactive position. Women can only shake up the patriarchal machinery, not effect change (33–40). Such a position ignores the insidious and powerful ability on the part of patriarchy to keep itself and its imaginary quest for power intact. No matter what women do, the patriarchy will condemn it to protect itself. Expressions of female power and attempts to invert the patriarchal order are often used to justify further and greater oppression. A recent example from popular culture illustrates this point. During the 1992 television season, a character named Murphy Brown decided to have a child outside wedlock. In a television show of the same name, Murphy Brown is a middle-aged, highly successful, and independent newswoman. Her pregnancy was unplanned, so her decision to have the baby would seem consistent with the conservative right's anti-choice views. It would appear that Brown was being a dutiful, patriarchal daughter. What resulted, however, was a condemnation by the conservative right, whose mouthpiece is former Vice-President Dan Quayle. He argued that Brown's decision "made a mockery of fatherhood." This example illustrates Irigaray's point: if women take control of their own desires and reproduction, under any circumstance, they are condemned. Nothing a woman does is right. But what I find so appealing about Irigaray's theories is her hope. In effect, she reassures women: let them condemn us, but let us not become discouraged; our very existence makes them anxious. Creating a stir, reacting, and speaking from female experience is always revolutionary, always a challenge to the oppressive structure.

Surprisingly, many have attacked Irigaray for being apolitical, almost too theoretical, unwilling to become involved in the political squalor. Elizabeth Grosz offers a succinct defense:

> Her interrogation of philosophical and psychoanalytic discourses, seeking their flaws and "blindspots," her use of paradigms against themselves is directed toward concrete political goals: the positive reinscription of women's bodies, the positive reconstruction of female morphologies, and thus the creation of perspectives, positions, desires that are inhabitable by women *as* women. (169)

Irigaray's emphasis on Marxism, moreover, represents a clear understanding of the economic and cultural difficulties women face:

> Woman has functioned most often by far as what is at stake in a transaction, usually rivalrous, between two men, her passage from father to husband included. She has functioned as merchandise. . . . Of course, commodities should never speak, and certainly should not go to market alone. For such actions turn out to be totally subversive to the economy of exchange among subjects. (*This Sex* 157–58)

Here Irigaray underscores her method for changing the oppressive status of women—speaking out, speaking up, violating the silence women have been forced to accept for centuries.

Further, what Felski calls reactive, Irigaray calls a respect for multiplicity:

> We haven't been taught, nor allowed, to express multiplicity. To do that is to speak improperly. Of course, we might—we were supposed to?—exhibit one "truth" while sensing, withholding, muffling another. . . . Veiling and unveiling: isn't that what interests them? What keeps them busy? Always repeating the same operation, every time. On every woman. (*This Sex* 210)

Judith Butler, who calls for a "coalitional feminism," echoes Irigaray: "Perhaps, paradoxically, 'representation' will be shown to make sense for feminism only when the subject of 'women' is nowhere presumed" (6). Simply put, such a strategy accounts for the shifting and often contradictory expectations patriarchy places upon women. Both Irigaray and Butler imply that such a dynamic strategy will keep patriarchal ideology guessing.

Irigaray's focus on the female body has caused just as much if not more debate than her views on language and political change. According to such critics, this emphasis is "essentialist" and only justifies further patriarchal oppression. For Irigaray, the female body in and of itself is enough to "jam the patriarchal machinery of oppression" (*This Sex* 78). Those who criticize her on this point often fail to account for the context of such statements. As I mentioned earlier, in psychoanalytic theory, the female genitals are constant reminders to the male that castration is a distinct possibility. In the Lacanian framework, the other, the entity that will bring psychic completion to the subject, is called the *phallus*. The equation with the literal penis is not something that Lacan argues for, but he implies that through the *méconnaissance* of existence that occurs during the subject's entrance into the symbolic, the subject often equates the penis with the phallus. Irigaray, then, seeks to retrieve the concept of the female body from this marginalized and degraded position.

> Irigaray does not oppose the phallus to a "raw" or "pure" female body; on the contrary, she demonstrates that the female body is the site for patriarchal power relations and, at the same time, for symbolic and representational resistances. (Grosz 144)

It is precisely such a reading that prompts Rose Braidotti to assert that "a feminist woman theoretician who is interested in thinking about sexual difference and the feminine today cannot afford not to be an essentialist" (93). Female bodies have been the site of male fantasies and manipulation for centuries. To value the female body and recognize the threat it poses to the patriarchy is an effective feminist strategy for political and cultural change.

The advantages of feminist psychoanalytic theory regarding questions concerning female representation and theatre cannot be ignored. Judith Roof, for example, defends psychoanalysis's appropriateness to feminist dramatic criticism:

> As a creative feminist practice that takes account of theoretical analysis, theatre has become the scene for a continued negotiation between feminism and psychoanalysis because of its general investment in spectacle, its community context, its generic resistance to alteration, and its obvious metaphorical connection to psychoanalysis. (324–25)

Further and in terms of this study, psychoanalysis offers a more suitable perspective on what constitutes the "real" for both feminism and drama. As is supported by the scholarship on the three authors, their methods in their later works often defy conventional dramatic classification, which has forced many critics to reach outside the dramatic vocabulary for accurate descriptions. Sam Shepard's dramatic techniques, for example, have been defined as super-realistic, defined in jazz and rock music terms and even in terms of the work of contemporary artist Robert Rauschenberg.[7] The later dramas of O'Neill and Pinter have also been described as neither realist, naturalist, nor absurdist, but as some combination of the three.[8] Psychoanalytic feminist theory, in particular, does not assume that a realistic representation of subjectivity necessitates a coherence of character, set, motives, or structure, but in fact argues against such a conception of realism. Though dramatic conventions have their place and they are not entirely ignored by these authors, they are displaced or decentered. Like their female characters, the dramatic structures of O'Neill, Pinter, and Shepard violate reductive classifications, perhaps as a result of their focus on the female in their plays. However, I do not mean to imply that as a result of their experimental forms they are participating in some form of feminine writing. Rather, their shifts in female characterization parallel shifts in form. And more often than not, actual women influenced their reconsiderations of their fictional representations of women.

The reluctance on the part of the female characters to play their parts in the plays of O'Neill, Pinter, and Shepard forces their male counterparts and their audiences to reevaluate the mechanisms which classify women stereotypically and consequently oppress females. The female characters resist occupying "a kind of Alaska," a metaphor I have borrowed from Harold Pinter to describe the objectified placement of women within patriarchal constructs. Many female characters in these plays resist being "iced over" by male expectations; they resist being transformed into mirrors for male desires. By focusing on the domestic setting and by creating female characters who resist the traditional, sexist roles in that setting, the three playwrights employ what Brecht defined as the *alienation effect*:

> What is involved here is, briefly, a technique of taking the human social incidents to be portrayed and labelling them as something striking, something that calls for explanation, is not to be taken for granted, not just natural. The object of this "effect" is to allow the spectator to criticize constructively from a social point of view. (125)

Throughout the plays of O'Neill, Pinter, and Shepard, the audience and the male characters are confronted with the female stereotypes they have taken for granted, only to find them misleading, inaccurate, and often displaced. Consequently, the plays force their audiences to reconsider such female classifications and perhaps alter their expectations and biases concerning the role of women in both the plays and the culture at large.

By focusing on the mature dramas of O'Neill, Pinter, and Shepard, as well as the dramas that contain their fullest expression of female characterization (even when these female characters do not appear on stage), I will demonstrate that these works dismantle cultural expectations regarding gender. And while my reading may be just as oppressive as Alejandra Pizarnik's sadistic countess, it is my hope that, through the use of Irigaray and others, I do not merely recast the female characters into icy mirrors to reflect my own cultural, feminist, or psychoanalytic expectations. By affording ambiguity, irony, and enigma to their female characters, the theorists, as well as the texts, make a place for women in drama, a genre that attempts, at least, to account for multiplicity, the multiple voices Irigaray argues is important to feminist projects.

2

"What Is a Man Without a Good Woman's Love?"
O'Neill's Madonnas

All is mirror!
    —Octavia Paz, "The Prisoner"

EUGENE O'NEILL studies are characterized by their frequent discussions concerning the relationship between O'Neill's own life and his dramas. Given the voluminous material available, as well as the frequent and compelling similarities between O'Neill's work and his life, it is almost impossible to avoid such discussions when approaching this playwright. O'Neill himself encouraged such comparison by frequently mentioning that his characters were created from his personal life. Three plays in particular are autobiographical: *The Iceman Cometh* (completed in 1939 but not produced until 1946), *Long Day's Journey into Night* (completed in 1941 but not produced until 1956), and *A Moon for the Misbegotten* (completed in 1943 but not produced until 1947).[1]

W. K. Wimsatt in *The Verbal Icon* cautions against the overuse of biographical details and authorial intention when he argues that "critical inquiries, unlike bet are not settled in this way. Critical inquiries are not settled by consulting the oracle" (18). While I do not wish to "consult the oracle" in order to answer critical questions, I do wish to look at O'Neill's life, particularly his relationship to women and the women's movement at the time, in order to establish his awareness of feminist issues before discussing these individual plays.

17

Born forty years after the meeting at Seneca Falls that began the feminist movement in America, O'Neill lived during an era in which women's equality became a national issue. Ethel Klein notes that between 1908 and 1925 over two hundred bills advocating women's rights reached Congress (13). According to Adele Heller and Lois Rudnick, this was the era of the New Woman:

> The New Woman was no longer bound by the separate spheres and assumed biological and intellectual limitations that kept her mother at home. She was presumably free to work, study, and determine her own life and sexual partners. During this period, middle-class women gained greater access to higher education and the professions. Working-class women, who often did not have the choice of staying at home, became actively involved in labor organizing, while African American women took leading roles in working for civil rights and educational reform for their people. . . . The fiction of Progressive Era women writers focused on new possibilities for women, as well as on the constraints that racial and class barriers placed on the New Woman. (4–5)

During his early years at the Provincetown Players, O'Neill associated with women who were clearly extraordinary even by New Woman standards: writers and activists Mabel Dodge, Neith Boyce, Susan Glaspell, and Dorothy Day, among others.

Although there is no evidence to suggest that O'Neill was directly involved in the women's rights movement, biographical details demonstrate that he not only valued his female counterparts but that he also encouraged their careers. One version, for example, of the Provincetown Players' discovery of Eugene O'Neill has it that playwright Neith Boyce and her husband, Hutchins Hapgood, read *Bound East for Cardiff*, and Boyce then sent it to George Cram Cook, the leader and founder of the influential theatre group (Gelb and Gelb 309). In another anecdote noted by Arthur and Barbara Gelb, O'Neill had a woman director for *The Rope*, Nina Moise, who offered her services to the Provincetown Players after seeing a rehearsal of Boyce's plays in which, she said, "the actors didn't know enough not to bump into one another" (qtd. in Gelb and Gelb 325). During rehearsals for *The Rope*, Moise suggested cuts and revisions. O'Neill, even at this early stage in his career was notorious for ignoring such suggestions. Despite his protests, however, he did execute the suggestions made by Moise (Gelb and Gelb 379–80).

A letter O'Neill wrote to Agnes Boulton is particularly telling. O'Neill mentions a conversation with George Tyler, an influential Broadway producer and friend of O'Neill and his father. They discuss Susan Glaspell, O'Neill's contemporary and a successful playwright:

> Tell Susan [Glaspell] I spoke to [George] Tyler about her play [*Inheritors* or *The Verge*, editors' note] and that he is genuinely eager to have a look at it. He said he had seen three of her plays at different times at the P. P. [Province-town Players]. . . . He said "that *girl* has a real touch of genius"—(he evidently thinks Susan is about as old as Helen Hayes), and he added with a questioning misgiving: "If the damned Greenwich Village faddists didn't get her into the radical magazine publications class." I didn't disillusion him about Susan being 19 and at the mercy of the faddist world—it was too funny—but I did say she was married to a very sensible man. Upon which Tyler heaved a sigh of relief and ceased to "view with alarm." (*Letters* 103, O'Neill's italics)

The anecdote is important because O'Neill not only ridicules Tyler's perceptions, but he also knows how to manipulate Tyler's sexist concerns. This renegade female, who later won a Pulitzer Prize for her play based on Emily Dickinson and who wrote what is now considered one of the finest examples of feminist literature, *Trifles* (1916), was not only married but married to a man who would keep her in line. Tyler's remarks, moreover, embody the ambivalence with which the feminist movement was received during the time. He paradoxically admires her ability while at the same time trivializing her ideas.

In their biography on O'Neill, the Gelbs note many instances suggesting that O'Neill shared this ambivalent attitude.
While he supported his female colleagues' advances in journal-
ism, literature, and drama, he had difficulty accepting their
sexual freedom and personal independence. O'Neill's expectations regarding the ideal wife were not only unrealistic but
required that she deny her own career, desires, and talents in
order to support his:

> He demanded an all but impossible ideal of wife-mistress-
> mother-secretary; a foil for his self-dramatization; a woman
> who could understand and appreciate him and devote
> herself entirely to his artistic aims. (Gelb and Gelb 369)

O'Neill's development as a playwright reflects this ambivalence, as well. In his first attempt at creating a female character,
Before Breakfast (1916), for example, the wife nags her husband
so much that he commits suicide. In *Abortion* (1914), a woman
has an abortion and dies, but it is her male partner who takes
center stage. The female character is merely the means by
which the male character becomes dramatic and interesting. In
Desire under the Elms (1924), however, O'Neill dramatizes a
couple who reestablish "their love so that they need to rely on
nothing outward" (Bogard 224). O'Neill focused on female representation even further in *Strange Interlude* (1928), calling it
his "woman play" (qtd. in Gelb and Gelb 589).

For many critics including the Gelbs and Travis Bogard,
O'Neill's representations of women remained stereotypical throughout his career, and all three point to O'Neill's mother as the
source of this mode of representation.[2] As a morphine addict,
Ella Quinlan O'Neill represented the extremes of both Madonna
and prostitute; her morphine addiction was then associated with
such women, not middle-class mothers. The character Jamie
Tyrone says as much in *Long Day's Journey into Night*. Such
criticism implies, then, that O'Neill could not reconcile this
contradictory maternal behavior, thereby creating a neurotic
energy that propelled him to the stage. However, such argu-

ments ignore the prevalence of feminine stereotypes throughout patriarchal culture. Furthermore, they elide the important distinction between the function of the whore and the prostitute within patriarchal systems of representation. Since these stereotypical roles are so prevalent in patriarchal culture and so important to my discussions of O'Neill, Pinter, and Shepard, they require clarification.

In her discussion concerning female representation, Luce Irigaray analyzes, explains, and demonstrates the motives behind the popularity of these stereotypical feminine roles within a patriarchal culture and especially their role in psychoanalysis. Her rationale for her emphasis on psychoanalysis and its relation to feminism is its ability to expose patriarchal ideology:

> Psychoanalytic discourse on female sexuality is the discourse of truth. A discourse that tells the truth about the logic of truth: namely, that *the feminine occurs only within models and laws devised by male subjects* (*This Sex* 86).

As a result of the imaginary's effect on the symbolic, the subject desires a return to the original jubilation experienced during the mirror stage. Representation becomes a re-presentation of oneself to oneself. This origin, of course, requires the cooperation and cooptation of the mother:

> Therefore, if you are a boy, you will want, as soon as you reach the phallic stage, to return to the origin, turn back toward that origin. That is, possess the mother, get inside the mother who is the place of origin, in order to reestablish continuity with it and to see and know what happens there. And moreover, to reproduce yourself there. If you are born a girl, the question is quite other. No return to, toward, inside the place of origin is possible unless you have a penis. The girl will herself be the place where origin is repeated, re-produced and reproduced, though this does not mean that she thereby repeats "her" original topos, "her" origin. On the contrary, she must break any contact with it, or with her, and making one last turn, by a kind of vault—up one *more* branch of the family tree—she must get to the

place where origin can be repeated *by being counted*.[3]
(*Speculum* 41)

In addition to arguing that this phallic economy prohibits
female desire as a result of the imaginary quest towards the
origin, Irigaray also indicates the important role women play in
this drama. As she argues later at great length, women serve as
objects of exchange in the phallic economy that gives paternity
supreme power.

Irigaray outlines the importance of the female roles, especially the roles of the mother, the virgin, and the prostitute in
patriarchal culture. Mothers

> are essential to its (re)production (particularly inasmuch as
> they are [re]productive of children and of the labor force:
> through maternity, child-rearing, and domestic mainte-
> nance in general). Their responsibility is to maintain the
> social order without intervening so as to change it. . . . *The
> virginal woman, on the other hand, is pure exchange value.*
> She is nothing but the possibility, the place, the sign of
> relations among men. . . . The *prostitute* remains to be
> considered. Explicitly condemned by the social order, she
> is implicitly tolerated. . . . In her case, the qualities of the
> female bodies are "useful." However, these qualities have
> "value" only because they have already been appropriated
> by a man, and because they serve as the locus of relations—
> hidden ones—between men. (*This Sex* 185–86)

Clearly, all roles deny female desire. Luce Irigaray and Jacques
Lacan define this role playing as "the masquerade of femininity." As both of Irigaray's books demonstrate, this ideology is
pervasive, but she also illustrates that there are women who do
"jam the patriarchal machinery" or, to use my metaphor, shatter
the glass or ice of the "Alaskan" mirror of female representation
and oppression. By expressing any desire that violates these
roles, women change their own position and the position of
women in general. Through such actions, women are unfaithful
to the law of the father, the law of patriarchy and paternity that
requires that women play the game. This strategy does not

imply, however, that there is an "other" feminist language, mode of representation, or discourse.

> Infidelity is *not* outside the system of marriage, the symbolic, patriarchy, but hollows it out, ruins it, from within. Unlike such infidelity, a new system, a feminist system, one constant, faithful to the tenets and dogmas of feminism would be but another Name-of-the-Father, feminism as a position and a possession. (Gallop, *Daughter's Seduction* 48)

This infidelity creates a space for women that does not deny their desire within the phallic economy. Gallop's point is an important one that distinguishes between the term *prostitute* and the term *whore*. I use the term *prostitute* to indicate women who fulfill men's sexual desires. I use *whore*, on the other hand, to indicate those female infidels who threaten the patriarchal system by their female desire.

However, such distinctions begin to blur in the later O'Neill plays. Female characters are both mothers and prostitutes, and this aggregate creates female characters who are unfaithful to traditional, stereotypical representations of women. Thus, O'Neill's mother, who was both, can be read not as the origin of his creative neurosis, but as an inspiration for more complex and sympathetic portrayals of femininity.

Furthermore, during the creation of these final plays, O'Neill was involved with Carlotta Monterey. While I do not wish to argue that she forced O'Neill to reconsider his female representations, some evidence suggests that she inspired him to reconsider his representations of women. Her assistance during these final years and plays is well known. In a note to Monterey upon the completion of *Mourning Becomes Electra*, O'Neill refers to her as his "collaborator" (qtd. in Gelb and Gelb 735).

That O'Neill discussed his ideas with her is clear from her knowledge of his original idea for his grand cycle of plays towards the end of his career, the cycle that led to his completion of *The Iceman Cometh*, *Long Day's Journey into Night*, and

A Moon for the Misbegotten. According to Travis Bogard, O'Neill began by toying with the idea of a character named Bessie Bowen who was based on a "career woman and industrialist . . . named Kate Gleason" (372). Bogard continues by arguing that this focus was a departure for O'Neill: Bessie, unlike Nina Leeds and Lavinia Mannon, who used their sexuality to destroy men, used "her financial acumen" (374). Carlotta Monterey, however, offers a different view regarding this scenario: "Gene wanted to write about different phases in the history of America. . . . How women entered the field of industry, how the great automobile empires evolved, about banking and shipping and the decline of the clippers" (qtd. in Gelb and Gelb 792). Monterey's assessment of the play clearly lacks the misogynistic overtones in Bogard's version, an absence that suggests Monterey's sympathy to and interest in female economic and personal power.

O'Neill's own attempts to reject the melodrama of his father's theatre may have also influenced his reconsideration of female representation throughout his career. In general, melodramas portrayed women as remarkably capable, but long-suffering and self-sacrificing, usually in order to represent traditional and sexist feminine roles. Women may have saved their families, lovers, and husbands from gruesome ends, but once indoors, they were often submissive to the very men they helped rescue (Rahill 225–97; Gledhill 33–36). While these conventions informed O'Neill's craft, his experiments with form and character throughout his career indicate his dissatisfaction with these traditional dramatic models. As Travis Bogard points out, O'Neill used these tactics "to shake his audiences from the spectator's habitual, lethargic 'suspended disbelief'" (xiv).

Bogard does not argue that O'Neill used this method to encourage his audiences to reconsider their expectations regarding women and female representation, but Judith Barlow's analysis of the drafts of *Long Day's Journey into Night* indicates that O'Neill was reconsidering and amending his representation of Mary Tyrone throughout the writing process. By the time he reached the final draft, he had "clearly moderated his original portrait of a viciously spiteful woman" (21). Further, according to Monterey's diaries, he was formulating *Long Day's Journey into Night* in 1939, just before he began *The Iceman* (qtd. in Bogard 427). This evidence suggests that O'Neill may have been aware of the limitations of his previous modes of female representation.

Whatever the motivation or authorial intent, the later O'Neill plays demonstrate the limits of such stereotypical representation of women, as well as the limits of patriarchal oppression of women. Perhaps the best way to describe the means by which O'Neill accomplishes this task in his later plays is through one final anecdote that not only says volumes about O'Neill, but also offers an apt illustration for Lacan's formulations regarding the mirror stage. According to one famous account, O'Neill habitually checked himself in mirrors, windows, and almost anything else that would reflect his image. Susan Glaspell's husband, George Cram Cook, confronted him on this narcissistic habit, saying, "You're the most conceited man I've ever known, you're always looking at yourself." O'Neill replied, "No, I just want to be sure I am here" (Sheaffer, *Son and Playwright* 239–40). O'Neill's comment articulates Lacan's conclusions concerning the male subject: he requires a mirror to ensure his existence.

In his later plays, O'Neill's male characters frequently require that women, both on stage and off, masquerade as women through stereotypical roles, thus giving to men a sense of personal power, identity, and autonomy. O'Neill's later plays demonstrate the process by which the male characters banish their female counterparts into "a kind of Alaska," a marginalized position that denies female desire and thereby creates a perfect looking glass for the men themselves. Since many of the female characters do not comply completely, O'Neill illustrates the cracks in the ice of stereotypical female representation.

The Iceman Cometh

With *The Iceman Cometh* (1946), O'Neill creates an urban, male wasteland, and through this nearly pristine representation of patriarchy, he illustrates the means by which it perpetuates itself and its fantasies. Women, both onstage and offstage, are vehicles for male desires. Issues concerning truth and illusion oscillate endlessly until the men in the play finally resolve to cling to their illusions. The decrepit surroundings serve only to heighten the wasteland image.

Much has been made regarding this dialectic of truth and illusion in the play.[4] It is difficult to ignore, since Larry brings it to our attention early in the play: "The lie of the pipe dream is what gives life to the whole misbegotten mad lot of us" (569–70). As the rest of the play demonstrates, this pipe dream is the dream of personal power; all the roomers, from Joe Mott to Larry Slade, believe they control their destinies. However, if we are tempted to believe that the characters would fare better if they would just face the truth about themselves, the play offers us Hickey, truth's traveling salesman who only offers emptiness.

O'Neill establishes this dialectic in order to expose its inherent illusory status. The quest for truth, particularly the truth about one's identity is futile. This thematic consideration is important when approaching the representation of women throughout the play. According to Jacques Lacan, Jacques Derrida, Luce Irigaray, Jane Gallop, and others, the tendency to dichotomize groups or categorize gender is a telltale sign of patriarchal oppression and discourse, what they label phallocentrism.[5] O'Neill's analysis of the truth-illusion dialectic, as well as the play's subsequent retreat from the dichotomy, indicates that O'Neill attempts to illustrate the limitations of such phallocentric ideology. For poststructuralist critics like Lacan, Derrida, and Irigaray, the attempt is in and of itself a method for disturbing this rigid ideology.

As mentioned earlier, the position of women within phallocentrism is that of an empty set. In her introduction to Jacques

Lacan's *Feminine Sexuality*, Jacqueline Rose argues that women, both real and fictional, occupy an absent-present position:

> As the place onto which lack is projected, and through
> which it is simultaneously disavowed, woman is a "symp-
> tom" for the man. Defined as such, reduced to being
> nothing other than this fantasamic place, the woman does
> not exist. . . . Within the phallic definition, the woman is
> constituted as "not all," in so far as the phallic function rests
> on an exception (the 'not') which is assigned to her. Woman
> is excluded *by* the very nature of words, meaning that the
> definition poses her as exclusion. Note that this is not the
> same thing as saying that woman is excluded *from* the
> nature of words. (48–49)

Like Luce Irigaray, Rose demonstrates that women are nothing
in the phallic economy. By highlighting the absence of women
and yet demonstrating the importance of the feminine via stereotypical female memories, as well as the prostitutes on stage,
Iceman aptly illustrates this paradox of the patriarchal paradigm.

Like *Strange Interlude* (1928), *Iceman* is a "choric drama"
(Bogard 414–16), but clearly it is a male chorus. While Travis
Bogard specifies that the chorus is made up of only Larry,
Parritt, and Hickey, the play illustrates that all the men are
singing the same song: pipe dreams or the lies by which the men
reassure themselves must be upheld at all costs.

More importantly, the play illustrates that this sense of
autonomy is ironically and ferociously upheld by the complicity
of a community. As Michael Manheim notes, "These people are
closest to one another when most comforted by their illusions
and farthest from one another when they are most insecure
about their illusions" (*Kinship* 150). Robert Brustein concurs,
arguing that the illusions insure inner peace:

> In this community, the price of mutual toleration is mutual
> silence. Actually this community is almost Utopian. Before
> Hickey comes, the men live in relative harmony together
> by adhering to a single doctrine—the doctrine of Tomor-

row—keeping hope alive through the anticipation of significant action on a day which never comes. (342)

Given the work of Lacan, Rose, and Irigaray, it would
appear that the men uphold their illusions so well that they do
not need the presence of the feminine. To use the mirror
metaphor, the men are so reliant upon the illusion of autonomy
that they are willing to serve as mirrors for one another. As the
play shows, however, casting women in stereotypical roles, even
when they are actually absent from the stage is crucial to the
perpetuation of this illusion. Larry's description of these pipe
dreams in the opening scene, moreover, indicates that gender
plays an important role in these male illusions. The men are
misbegotten, mistakes of birth.

From a feminist perspective, the play is extremely compelling. Through the male characters' manipulation of the offstage
female, O'Neill clearly shows how men create feminine fantasies
in order to exist. The play quickly establishes this process and its
benefits through the absent character of Bessie Hope. We meet
her just after Harry has come out of his drunken slumber. When
he criticizes his colleagues for allowing him to fall asleep in a
chair "like a bum" (592), his brother-in-law Mosher and their
friend McGloin defend themselves by invoking Bessie's name: "It
was one of those nights when memory brought poor old Bessie
back to you" (592). Hope responds with a melodramatic flourish:

> Yes, that's right, boys. I remember now. I could almost see
> her in every room just as she used to be—and it's twenty
> years since she—(*His throat and eyes fill up. A suitable
> sentimental hush falls on the room*). (592)

By juxtaposing this awakening scene to Harry's retelling of the
myth of Bessie, the play illustrates the advantages of an absent
female—Harry can manipulate his memory of her in order to
support his present pipe dreams or, in this case, his present
state of sloth. Like a quick shot of whiskey, the pipe dream
enables the disoriented Harry to cope with reality. Ironically,
Hope gains a sense of identity by playing his lack: he has lost the

Madonna who completed his life, but this lack allows him to play the complete role of the grieving husband. He need not take any responsibility for his actions, since he is so overcome with grief. The play highlights the illusory status of this process through the satiric stage directions, Hope's own melodramatic tone, and later Larry's comments on the "drama" that Harry has just performed. As Larry tells Parritt, "Isn't a pipe dream of yesterday a touching thing? By all accounts, Bessie nagged the hell out of him" (592). This truth about Bessie Hope, however, is also stereotypical; she is a nagging fishwife. Such a depiction silences Bessie as effectively as her death. As Jane Gallop notes, the oppressed position of women does not imply that they literally do not speak—though it often does. Instead, when women do speak, their words are trivialized (*Body* 71).

In another story about Bessie, the men recount the time they "got the better" of this nagging, upstart woman. In this narrative, they depict Bessie as a tightwad. They criticize her for not being more like a prostitute; she is too prudish. More importantly, Bessie's control of the finances violates her position as an object of exchange in the phallic economy. She clearly oversteps patriarchal bounds. Their quick change routine is meant to humiliate and remind Bessie that commodities have no rights within the patriarchal economy. Men have power. The narrative dispels the feminine threat. Though some might call this memory mere comic relief, that the men need to tell a story in which they triumph over the nagging Bessie suggests that the mere mention of her name produces enough anxiety in this illusory community to warrant further female objectification.

The absent character of Marjorie Tomorrow functions similarly. Marjorie, however, threatens the patriarchal system further because she was not duped by a practical joke. She committed adultery. In this masculine haven, however, even this action is manipulated into a mirror for Jimmy Tomorrow. Jimmy Tomorrow defines her as a whore, the sexually driven destructive female who expresses female desire. He then gains a sense of being a good man who narrowly escaped the clutches of such a woman. His drinking reflects his goodness; she no longer exists in his alcoholic haze. Any threat to his identity is diminished through this process.

Like Jimmy, Don Parritt casts his mother, Rosa, into a similar role. Through her activity in politics, she violates Parritt's expectations regarding motherhood. He not only condemns her because of her personal failings, but also because her involvement violates the American way.

Even the setting reflects these limited representations of femininity. On the one hand, the saloon is a patriarchal paradise: the men escape from their whorish women to the company of men. On the other, the bar appears womblike; there are few distractions, no light, and enough fluid to keep the men alive. The result is similar to Brecht's alienation effect. The familiar is made unfamiliar through the decay: the "old boy network" appears to be the "dead boy network."

The women who do appear in the play initially do not cause any disturbance in the delicate balance of masculine illusions and the dualistic perceptions of female illusions that underlie and uphold these fantasies. They are prostitutes, not whores, women who serve rather than disturb male expectations. She, like the Madonna, does not have "*any right to her own pleasure*" (Irigaray, *This Sex* 187). When the prostitutes in the play speak, moreover, their utterances are consistent with the men's pipe dreams regarding women. Cora, for instance, says she wants to settle down and raise kids and cows. She is a prostitute who dreams of becoming a Madonna.

More importantly, when the women enter the bar, they must unsex themselves. Harry makes this qualification clear:

> Never thought I'd see the day when Harry Hope's would have tarts rooming in it. What'd Bessie think? But I don't let 'em use my rooms for business. And they're good kids. Good as anyone else. (599–600)

Harry's comment illustrates the female dualism that permeates the play: women like Bessie and women like the prostitutes are mutually exclusive. In addition, with their sexuality, any sexuality deposited at the door, they cannot disturb the status quo; they are "one of the boys," full of dreams and whiskey.

In *Speculum of the Other Woman*, Luce Irigaray illustrates the limits of this line of reasoning, exposing the myth of sameness or the old dream of symmetry that presumes that men and women are the same. The context in which she makes her remarks is Freudian. In his formulations concerning the development of human sexuality, Freud establishes the differences between male and female development, then imposes the same model of sexual development onto women, whom he has previously defined as "other," and subsequently faults the feminine for not adhering to the masculine model. The conclusion for both Freud and patriarchy is not that the model might be defective, but that women are. If women would only listen to men, the system would work; they would see that they are the same as men, fit the same model, have the same desires (*Speculum* 26–27). This myth, then, does not assure equality, only a theoretical method for justifying oppression.

As the prostitutes indicate in their dealings with Rocky, they are nothing more than a vehicle through which men may deal with one another; they are commodities. The play clearly illustrates that the money from the "johns" does not stay with the women but is passed on to Rocky to confirm his phallic power.

> The law that orders our society is the exclusive valorization of men's needs/desires, of exchanges among men. What the anthropologist calls the passage from nature to culture thus amounts to the institution of the reign of hom(m)o-sexuality. (Irigaray, *This Sex* 171)

In other words, women serve only to establish relationships among men, hence the term *hom(m)o-sexuality*; even when they are characterized as "one of the boys," they are merely upholding the phallic economy.

There is one minor but significant exception to this depiction of the onstage women. During Hickey's confession, he mentions that the prostitutes he visited enjoyed his jokes. Cora, who has had her Madonna illusions stripped away by Hickey, interjects at this moment in his speech, saying, "Jees, all de lousy jokes I've had to listen to and pretend was funny" (697). This interruption creates a gap in both Hickey's monologue and the play's overall representation of these onstage women. During this moment, Cora is not "one of the boys"; she has her own desires. The play exposes her for what she is—a woman who must masquerade for men and deny those desires. The inhabitants of the bar ignore Cora's interjections, and by the end of the play, she returns to her "normal" behavior. Through the process of unveiling female desire, albeit slight, however, O'Neill illustrates the "kind of Alaska" these women inhabit within a patriarchal system.

Hickey's arrival shatters the illusory equilibrium of Harry Hope's much more drastically. It would appear that Hickey brings truth about identity and gender. Hickey's arrival does serve as an effective dramatic device to these ends, for through his interactions with the other characters, the play exposes the fictional nature of the men's narratives and perceptions of female characters. In some ways, through Hickey the play shatters the "Alaska" the women have been forced to occupy throughout the men's narratives. Madonnas are shown to be blemished, and whores like Marjorie Tomorrow are shown to be justified in their actions. None of the absent women are exactly what her male counterpart wanted her to be. The effect of these revelations is disastrous: the men's mirrors are so shattered that even the whiskey, their liquid mirror, will not work.

With Hickey's departure, however, Harry, Jimmy, and the others encase the more complicated realities of the feminine once again. They ignore the anxiety these realities produce, and they continue pursuing their pipe dreams and their myth of masculine autonomy. They end as they began. Because O'Neill exposes the machinery of female objectification, the play demonstrates that the male characters, motivated by the need for personal power, construct illusory feminine characters through their memories. But the roles are socially imposed, not the result of "natural" female difference or sexuality. In this way, all the men are "icemen" who ice over the threat that femininity poses in order to make mirrors of their female counterparts.

As Hickey's confession illustrates, he has not entirely removed his misconceptions of femininity from his own life. During this speech, Hickey describes Evelyn as a Madonna, the archetypal good wife and mother. Though Hickey initially admires and loves the image of himself this maternal mirror reflects, the difficulties such a role poses for men and women are clearly illustrated throughout the rest of his confession. Evelyn's Madonna role offers no place for female sexuality; sex and virtue are mutually exclusive. Hickey's response was to seek solace in prostitutes who afforded him a mirror for his sexual fantasies. He even mentions that he wished Evelyn could be more like those women he paid to laugh at his jokes.

Sexual desire violates the mutually exclusive categories of female behavior that Hickey has internalized. He wants both Madonna and prostitute embodied in the same woman. Such a desire shatters his illusions about himself; the mirror will not reflect: "I got so I'd curse myself for a lousy bastard every time I saw myself in the mirror" (699).

Throughout the course of his confession, however, Hickey becomes more confused by his ideology of femininity. He initially tells the roomers that he killed Evelyn for her own good to put her out of her misery and thereby to transform her into a Madonna or a saint. He, of course, inadvertently tells too much:

> I remember I stood by the bed and suddenly I had to laugh. I couldn't help it, and I knew Evelyn would forgive me. I remember I heard myself speaking to her, as if it was something I'd always wanted to say: "Well you know what you can to with your pipe dream now you damned bitch!" (700)

On the one hand, Hickey's response to Evelyn demonstrates the limits of the Madonna role for the male subject. Evelyn's forgiveness, loyalty, and sexual naïveté do not reassure Hickey; these qualities only remind him of his limitations, his existential lack. On the other, Hickey blames Evelyn for not living up to his contradictory expectations regarding femininity. Here the play drastically illustrates women's "no win" or "not all" position. Hickey wants both Madonna and whore, but he would resent Evelyn no matter which role she played. Rather than examining these confused gender roles, Hickey justifies his actions by defining Evelyn as a whore who has desires of her own. She, too, has a pipe dream. She wants him to live up to her expectations of him, another clear violation of female objectification.

Following his outburst, Hickey cannot accept the new version of Evelyn he has created, and like the other dreamers, he retreats to his original image of his absent female: "No! That's a lie! I never said—! Good God, I couldn't have said that! If I did, I'd gone insane! Why I loved Evelyn better than anything in life" (701). For Hickey, a life without the maternal mirror is a life of insanity, tellingly, a life where he loses himself, or rather, his perception of himself.

The one exception to this patriarchal process is Larry Slade. As O'Neill's lengthy stage notes indicate, the physical positions of the dreamers reflect their existential states that shift throughout the course of the play. At the opening of the play, Larry is content with his "grandstand" existence, but his physical position inside the group makes it clear that he, like the others, relies on the community of dreamers to perpetuate his illusion. In the final scene, however, the roomers are jubilantly celebrating the return of their pipe dreams, while Larry sits at a table alone near a window musing over the play's events.

Like the other men, Larry has a woman in his past who has not lived up to his expectations. And like the other men, he seeks refuge from this female threat through the comfort of the saloon. Unlike the other men, however, Larry does not cast Rosa Parritt into any of the socially constructed feminine roles. As he says, he is doomed to see "both sides of the question" in the political movement (580), but this vision also extends to his view of Rosa. While Parritt attempts to justify his betrayal of Rosa through culturally approved stereotypes, Larry does not resort to such justification.

Larry's encouraging Parritt to commit suicide could be read as Larry's own perception of Rosa as a Madonna of the movement whom he must protect and keep on a pedestal in order to achieve a sense of autonomy, but given Larry's comments about Rosa throughout the play, it is difficult to believe that he casts her in such a role. Instead, his response to Parritt defends Rosa's rights to live her life as she chooses and condemns Parritt's attempts to legislate her behavior. As Larry's comments and Parritt's suicide indicate, such a defense requires an enormous sacrifice for a man within the patriarchal system.

Larry says that he is "the only real convert to death Hickey has made here" (710), and in many ways, he is. By removing himself from the patriarchal ideologies that permeate the play and the lives of the roomers, Larry no longer participates in the pipe dream that "gives life to the whole misbegotten mad lot of us." The play does not indicate that Larry means his own death, but rather, it leaves us with a vision of Larry who remains in the bar but is now in the "grandstand," removed from the dreamers. He does not entirely divorce himself from the phallic system by leaving the bar, but he now inhabits it differently than he did at the play's outset. He sits near a window, but he does not look at it. Such a gesture, albeit subtle, reflects Larry's rejection of the looking glass. Admittedly, the play does not codify the results of Larry's decision into a thematic product. In this way, O'Neill violates the expectations regarding closure and completeness thereby creating a gap in our own theatrical and literary expectations, perhaps in the hopes that we, too, will consider the effects of existence without female oppression.

Long Day's Journey into Night

While O'Neill's *Iceman Cometh* illustrates the limitations of patriarchy through its absent women, *Long Day's Journey into Night* (1956) uses the onstage mother, Mary Tyrone, as well as numerous offstage mothers to illustrate these limitations. As in *The Iceman Cometh*, *Long Day's Journey* depicts the process of gender relations: the formation and codification of sex roles as well as the disastrous effects of such roles on both the women and the men in the play. The play's title highlights O'Neill's emphasis on process, and while process is important in *The Iceman Cometh*, as well, the use of process within the family setting is an important shift for O'Neill in the later play. Raymond Williams argues that a focus on process in general in *Long Day's Journey* marks a turning point in O'Neill's career:

> What comes out elsewhere [in O'Neill's works] as a conclusion—the sense of deadlock, of isolation, of insubstantial and destructive relationships—comes out here as a process: not those of static forms dramatized, as a single act, but their complex formation pressed deeply into a consciousness which is controlling convention. (294)

For Harold Bloom, *Long Day's Journey* poses a threatening vision of the family:

> The helplessness of family love to sustain, let alone heal, the wounds of marriage, of parenthood, and of sonship, have never been so remorselessly and so pathetically portrayed, and with a force of gesture too painful ever to be forgotten by any of us. (8)

While most would agree with Bloom on the play's effectiveness, his comment epitomizes one of the major difficulties with its reception. In Bloom's commentary, "marriage," "parenthood," and "sonship" imply the maternal, but nowhere is that expressly stated. Mary Tyrone's struggles, pain, and power are absent. In Bloom's commentary, Mary Tyrone appears to occupy the Lacanian empty set. Geraldine Fitzgerald, who inaugurated the role of Mary Tyrone on Broadway, indicates that this perspective was also prevalent during the play's first production when she was criticized for her portrayal of the character. Audiences and critics said, "You can't do this to Mary Tyrone. You can't make

her be so satirical and witty and needling of everybody on stage.
This cannot be. This is a sacred figure" (292). These responses to
the character of Mary accurately reflect the position of women
in patriarchal culture. Whether they are sanctified or dismissed, female characters are not given center stage. From
Aristotle on, female characters could not be tragic. They must
occupy the position of nothing in order to uphold patriarchal
expectations on the part of their fictional male counterparts and
their audiences. Motherhood is particularly "off limits."

Motherhood, however, is the central issue of *Long Day's
Journey*. The problem with Mary Tyrone, though, is that she is
not merely a maternal stereotype. Like the great male tragic
figures, she errs and suffers. Consequently, she is the dramatic
center of the play. Furthermore, the play contains numerous
references to offstage mothers, from the Virgin Mary, human-
ity's sacred mother in the Catholic doctrine, to James Tyrone's
Irish immigrant mother.

For Freud and Lacan, the centrality of the mother figure in
both the oedipal process and the mirror stage is crucial but
ambivalent. The mother at once serves as the mirror for male
desire, propelling him into culture and setting the agenda for
heterosexual relationships within the phallic economy. This
importance led Lacan to the concept of the *phallic mother*.
Simply, the mother has what the child does not—the father's
phallus. She is also the means by which the child returns to the
origin to attain his sense of autonomy. But for all of her usefulness, she is also the site of great ambivalence. First, her own
castration threatens the male child with his own. And second,
her role as absolute Madonna-mirror is complicated by the
child's realization that she has had sex with the father, prostituted herself to the father, or, more importantly, prostituted
the child's desire for an all-consuming love.

To resolve this ambivalence, the child must successfully
resolve the oedipal conflict. At that time, the child recognizes
that any phallic power the mother might presume is actually
borrowed from the father, the law of patriarchal culture.

> Through the "name-of-the-Father," the child is positioned
> beyond the structure of dual imaginary relations [with the
> mother] within the broader framework of culture, where
> genuine exchange may become possible (exchange requires
> the third term, the object exchanged between the subject
> and the other). However, the resolution of the oedipus
> complex or the assumption of the name-of-the-father is
> rarely if ever entirely successful. The imaginary returns,
> being only partially or unsuccessfully repressed, resurfac-
> ing in both pathological and "normal" forms in adult life as
> symptoms, dreams, and amorous relations, in those relations
> where the self strives to see itself in the other. (Grosz 47)

Within the phallic economy, women are objectified as mere
objects of exchange. With the influence of the imaginary relationship, however, the desire to attain autonomy through the
maternal mirror remains a potent and powerful force. The
concept of the phallic mother, then, is yet another paradoxical
formulation within the phallic economy. As mirror for the male,
she appears to wield a great deal of power. Through her the male
achieves his sense of autonomy, but in order to play this role, the
woman must deny her own desires or occupy "a kind of Alaska"
in order to have any worth whatsoever in this patriarchal
system.

Unlike the beginning of *The Iceman Cometh*, in *Long Day's
Journey*, O'Neill opens with reassuring images. In fact, the
play's opening could easily be taken from O'Neill's light, comic
family drama *Ah Wilderness!* (1933). Initially the family looks
conventional enough, remarkably at ease with one another. Gone
are the skid row bums, the decrepit surroundings, the tarts and
alcohol; instead, a family vacations at their New England sum-
mer home. Mary and James Tyrone joke and tease one another
about domestic matters. With their defenses down and their familial expectations raised, audiences are brought into the play.

> The images it [*The Iceman Cometh*] projects disturb the
> audience and makes them sharply aware of the contradic-
> tions normally thrust aside in the activity of daily living.

Those of *Long Day's Journey Into Night* take the audience into their very selves. (Chothia 143)

The setting will not allow audiences to dismiss the gender relations here, for these characters appear to be normal, just like us.

The men in the play appear sympathetic to Mary's condition at the outset. They seem to place Mary's health and desires before their own, thereby honoring the sanctified position of the mother in patriarchy. As the confessions in the last act reveal, however, this generosity of spirit is motivated by their own desire to have Mary return to her stereotypical role of mother in the household. During James's confession, for example, he tries to discredit Mary and cast himself in a better light. He tells Edmund that Mary's virginal past is a pipe dream, that she was, in fact, a flirt. Nowhere is the law of the father made more explicit in the play. While the boys struggle with their perceptions of Mary, James presumes to know Mary completely. He not only objectifies her through this assessment, but he presumes a privileged relationship to the object, which even the object does not have. In other words, he supposes to know her better than she knows herself.

Further, his misreading of Mary ignores the reality of the feminine masquerade within a patriarchal system.

The characteristics of femininity Freud outlines [in his essay on the castration complex]—seductive, coquettish behavior, narcissism, vanity, jealousy, and a weaker sense of justice—are a consequence of her acceptance of her lack (of the phallus). They are strategies developed to ensure that, even if she doesn't *have* the phallus, she may *become* the phallus, the object of desire for the other. (Grosz 132, Grosz's italics)

Far from being a contradiction, then, Mary's behavior is consistent with her role as mirror. James's assessment of Mary is motivated by the fact that his wife-mirror has begun to crack, and rather than examining his own need for such a mirror, James blames Mary. In this way, James casts himself in the role of the subject supposed to know, Lacan's definition of the male who presumes he is the phallus (*Feminine Sexuality* 139). Mary's behavior, however, is a threat to this powerful status. James relieves his discomfort through his memories of his dead mother. As he tells Edmund, he was the sole provider in the family, but during one Christmas, his mother had enough money to create a Dickensian version of the holiday. He concludes the tale reverentially: "A fine, brave, sweet woman. There never was a braver or finer" (808).

The rumors of suicide that surround James's father's death make such conclusions regarding his mother problematic. I do not mean to imply that James's mother drove her husband to suicide. Instead, because of his denial of the rumors, James appears to have a remarkable capacity for denial and revisionist readings of the past. In this way, the play undercuts James's assumption of patriarchal power and illustrates the familial issues James must ignore in order to attain and retain his sense of power. James's idealization of his mother, moreover, illustrates the illusion he hopes Mary will fulfill. Given these expectations, it is not difficult to see that Mary crumbled under them.

Jamie's response to Mary is one of the more desperate ones in the play. His need for the feminine mirror is made clear when he tells Edmund: "What is a man without a good woman's love? A God-damned hollow shell" (815). Like James, he turns to another woman when the maternal mirror cracks, but unlike James, he turns to a prostitute, the opposite extreme of femininity in patriarchy. His treatment of the prostitute, however, illustrates the extent to which Jamie's identity is dictated by female stereotypes. Since his mother has a whorish morphine habit, he treats the prostitute Fat Violet like a mother. With these female divisions blurred, Jamie's sense of self dissolves. "There is no vision of beatitude for Jamie. . . . His need is always beside him, in Mary, but he cannot reach her. Like Tantalus, he has no refuge from desire. His is the howl of a soul lost in hell" (Bogard 437).

Like Jamie, Edmund responds to Mary's condition by seeking another mirror, but unlike James and Jamie, he does not look to another woman. Instead, he looks to the great symbolic mother, the sea. Through his travels, he experiences the jubilant sense of the mirror stage; he, the sea, and the symbolic mother are unified, powerful, exuberant (811–12). During the course of this speech, however, Edmund realizes that his image is illusory. Unlike many of the other male characters, Edmund understands that such experiences are fantastic, illusory, imaginary. He does not presume knowledge, like his father; he does not function as the subject supposed to know. He concludes by saying, "You are alone, lost in the fog again, and you stumble on toward nowhere, for no good reason!" (812).

Perhaps in response to Jamie's inarticulate howl, Edmund tackles the word, the linguistic system that prohibits female desire and pleasure. He may not be able to construct meaning, but he continues to compose and explore. As he tells James, "Stammering is the native eloquence of us fog people" (812–13). Through the speech, O'Neill constructs an example of such stammering: Edmund shifts from jubilation to cynicism, from life to death, from self-understanding to self-doubt, from certitude to doubt regarding his abilities and language's abilities to communicate his experiences. The speech offers no answers, but it does express a sense of the decentered human condition; and more importantly, it does communicate. I do not mean to imply that Edmund has entered the feminine, a world in which the laws of patriarchal or phallocentric logic are violated, but through this speech, the play effectively illustrates the paradox of existence and discourse: we can dream of meaning, but we must remember, too, that disruption exists. Certitude is a dream.

The play challenges such certitude through the character of Mary Tyrone. O'Neill explicates Mary's life even before the men's confessions. By structuring the play in this way, O'Neill privileges the female narrative. As Mary's memories indicate, she began her life typically. She attended Catholic schools and played the part of the dutiful, virginal daughter. When her father brought James Tyrone into the house, Mary read the paternal message correctly. Here was a man her father thought worthy. Consistent with the typical patriarchal scenario, Mary could not have her father as a love object, so instead, she served as an object of exchange between men, thereby gaining a phallus of her own through her marriage to James Tyrone.

While Mary appears to have played the phallic game, she remembers that her mother opposed the marriage. According to Freud's theories of female sexual development, the difference of opinion is a natural occurrence in the process. The female subject must turn away from her mother as love object, and throughout this process, hostilities between mother and daughter ensue (183–93).

Irigaray, however, puts it another way. In the sexual marketplace where women are merely objects of exchange, they not only have no desire, but they are prohibited from relationships with one another. To put it in practical terms, women must compete with one another for the man's attention, since they cannot exist without being defined in some way by their relationship to the male subject (*This Sex* 170–97). Mary's own remarks indicate that she resents her mother's interference with her participation in this exchange. The mother-daughter relationship is further complicated because the mother is supposed to socialize the daughter in patriarchy. The female subject blames the mother for making her inferior, and this hostility propels the girl into culture, just as the castration complex propels the boy. Irigaray, again, takes this process one step further from a feminist perspective. Because of the mother's role in socialization, the daughter is taught to deny her own desires in order to attain value in the sexual marketplace. During an imaginary conversation with the mother, Irigaray accuses her mother, saying: "I swallowed ice. And here I am now frozen" (*One Doesn't Stir* 60). More importantly, the mother who has denied her own desires often uses the female child to vent her own frustrations. As Grosz states, it is not the mother per se that causes the difficulty but, instead, the limited roles patriarchy imposes: "The constricted suffocating motherhood is not the result of the mother's phallic lack, but an excess that can find no other social avenue or validated outlet" (182).

Mary's response to these complex feelings and contradictory expectations is to turn to the ultimate mother, the Virgin Mary of her Catholic faith. In many ways, her decision only creates further confusion. Constructed by the patriarchal church, this female figure embodies the patriarchal ideals regarding the virgin and the mother. The Virgin Mary perpetuates patriarchy and the Christian faith, but she does so without any sexuality. Like the prostitutes in *The Iceman Cometh*, she is completely unsexed. Such characterization diffuses any threat of female sexuality or the castrated female genitals. Mary's obsession with this figure, of course, illustrates her own ambivalence about her sexuality. Mary's suffering, however, may indicate the disastrous consequences of such an impossible female ideal. As a human, not a divine, woman, Mary must experience sex in order to procreate and perpetuate the patriarchy. In many ways, Mary's morphine addiction is similar to the behavior of the nineteenth-century hysterics, those female patients that Freud and Josef Bruer tried to cure and whose illnesses actually brought about the beginning of psychoanalysis. Feminists today argue that hysteria was a feminist response to patriarchy. Defined as sexual objects but prohibited desire in the patriarchy, these women resisted their oppression with their bodies (Hunter 89–118). Mary Tyrone's morphine addiction, then, could be read as her violation of these expectations.

In this way, Mary's movement away from the men in the play could reflect her desire to salvage some aspect of her desire. Mary's choice to pray to the Virgin Mary and not one of the paternal deities does mark a shift in her previous participation in patriarchy. Having retreated from the men in the play, Mary reaches out to another woman, a tendency that she also shares with the hysterics, notably Bertha Pappeheim who abruptly left treatment and subsequently became a feminist (Hunter

89–118). Though such a happy conclusion does not occur with Mary, she does reach out to the other female characters in the play. She does not succeed with the offstage cook, Bridget, but she does seem to make contact with the onstage maid, Cathleen. For Jean Chothia, Cathleen is a dramatic type, "the conventional comic servant of the nineteenth-century theatre. . . . She has not sufficient intrinsic interest to intrude on our impression of the family's isolation and, by the same token, can serve as the mirror in which the public face of each is reflected." Admittedly, Cathleen mirrors Mary's image of herself, "a considerate mistress and loving mother" (175), but she does listen to Mary in a way the men do not, particularly Edmund who is continually telling her to keep quiet. Mary's return to her past is also filled with memories of her relationships with the nuns, and she even admits that she considered joining a convent at one time. Surprisingly, it is a nun who encourages her to experience life and men and perhaps her own sexuality before considering a convent. Mary's dream-memory, moreover, is one in which she played the piano, expressed herself, and lived in a world of women. Such a dream is certainly idealized, and I do not mean to imply that by retreating to morphine and the Virgin Mary, Mary Tyrone represents a feminist solution to the conflicting stereotypes that oppress her, but her movement toward a community of women and away from the male community in which she currently resides is noteworthy. If nothing else, it indicates the level of her oppression: beleaguered by male expectations, Mary dreams of a female utopia. And in the dream, Mary has desires, desires that are not permitted by the phallic economy.

However, this dream is not enough to sustain Mary, and by the end of the play, illusion enshrouds her. She, who has been searching for her glasses throughout the play, is now shattered glass. She yearns for something to make her feel complete:

> What is it I'm looking for? I know it's something I lost. . . .
> Something I need terribly. I remember when I had it I was
> never lonely nor afraid. I can't have lost it forever, I would

die if I thought that. Because there would be no hope.
(825–26)

Here Mary articulates the fragmented nature of her existence, the break between her desires and those of the culturally imposed stereotypes of feminine behavior.

According to Irigaray, feminine "commodities" are essentially divided. But unlike the Lacanian split subject, which has access to the dominant system of illusory unity, the feminine subject is always split by this dominant, hierarchical discourse:

> Once again there is a schism between the two [the commodities' bodies and their bodies on the sexual market]. Two sides, two poles, nature and society are divided, like the perceptible and the intelligible, matter and form, the empirical and the transcendental. . . . The commodity, like the sign, suffers from metaphysical dichotomies. Its value, its truth, lies in the social element. But this social element is added on to its nature, to its matter, and the social subordinates it as a lesser value, indeed as non-value. Participation in society requires that the body submit itself to a specularization, a speculation, that transforms it into a value-bearing object, a standardized sign, an exchangeable signifier, a "likeness" with reference to an authoritative model. *A commodity—a woman—is divided into two irreconcilable "bodies"*: her "natural" body and her socially valued, exchangeable body, which is a particularly mimetic expression of masculine values. No doubt these values also express "nature," that is, the expenditure of physical force. But this latter—essentially masculine, moreover—serves for the fabrication, the transformation, the technization of natural productions. (*This Sex* 179–80)

Mary searches for a sense of herself and her body that eludes the social construction of Madonna and whore. What she obsessively talks about at the end of the play is the moment at which she became a fabrication, her meeting with James Tyrone, her initiation as an object on the sexual economy. At this point, the familial narrative also ruptures and closes down, ending with a frightening image. During this final scene, Mary is no longer herself. She is strangely youthful, her face "a marble mask of girlish innocence," carrying the wedding gown that signifies her movement into the realm of commodity (823–24). As the play chillingly demonstrates, this mask removes Mary from herself and those around her; she is literally entombed in this early image of herself, a symbol that represents the extremes of the patriarchy's perception and legislation of motherhood.

A Moon for the Misbegotten

While casting women in stereotypical roles produces disastrous results in *The Iceman Cometh* and *Long Day's Journey into Night*, *A Moon for the Misbegotten* (1947) offers a problematic alternative to such casting. Through the struggles and sacrifices of the main female character, Josie, the play illustrates the nature of the female masquerade in patriarchy. In this play, O'Neill explicitly creates a female character who clearly and consciously takes on the role of the Madonna in order to alleviate the suffering of another human being, the tortured Jamie Tyrone. While such a representation does not violate the stereotypical casting of women, it movingly illustrates the difficulties that women face when accepting such roles. Moreover, the play emphasizes the artificiality of such constructs.

For Luce Irigaray, who is skeptical about modes of female representation that attempt to establish themselves outside discourse and masculine modes (an attempt that Irigaray indicates is not even possible), the manipulation of the masquerade is an important way in which women can "jam the patriarchal machinery." She argues that

> for woman it is not a matter of installing herself within this lack, this negative, even by denouncing it, nor of reversing the economy of sameness by turning the feminine into the *standard for "sexual difference"*; it is rather a matter of trying to practice that difference. (*This Sex* 159)

O'Neill accomplishes this task in a method similar to that of *The Iceman Cometh* and *Long Day's Journey into Night*. He first establishes audience expectations and then thwarts them through a series of reversals and qualifications. *Moon*, however, may be the best example of this technique. As several critics have noted, the play itself is an odd combination of dramatic conventions. James Robinson argues that it is the most artificial of all the late plays (62). Michael Manheim, however, reads the use of melodramatic techniques, in particular, as a reflection of O'Neill's final dissatisfaction with the dramatic mode of his father. He notes that when the suicidal Jamie praises the work of the famous theatre director and playwright, David Belasco, O'Neill is calling for the dawn of a "new theatre" that moves beyond melodrama ("Transcendence" 157). Years after the completion of *Moon*, O'Neill admitted that it was the play he liked least (Bogard 452). This dissociation may have been prompted by O'Neill's reluctance to challenge the law of his theatrical father, or it may have been prompted by O'Neill's own failure to create a new dramatic form.

Given the complex portrayal of O'Neill's women in *The Iceman Cometh* and *Long Day's Journey into Night*, the character of Josie is problematic and is reminiscent of the female heroines of melodrama. Through O'Neill's opening description of her, for example, she appears to be a grotesque symbol for an idealized maternal force, much like the mother sea Edmund describes in *Long Day's Journey into Night*. Set in a house without roots, Josie serves as the play's "birthing center," the origin of new life and hope. She opens the play by helping her brother, Mike, begin his new life apart from her father's infertile, rocky farm, just as she helped her other brothers, Thomas and John. And while her father appears upset with her activities, he is not really upset with his sons' departures. Their making their mark on the world ensures the continuation of patriarchy. In this way, the play establishes Josie as the good mother.

Josie's familiarity with and participation in female roles is clearly established. As Michael Hinden succinctly notes, Josie is a virgin who pretends to be a whore, the reversal of James's image of his mother" (243). Interestingly, however, Josie's masquerade of femininity is itself shown to be a masquerade. By playing the role of prostitute, Josie cleverly removes herself from the sexual economy that the phallic system demands women participate in. As virgin, she would have become enmeshed in this system; as nonparticipatory prostitute, she is left alone by many of the men in the town.

O'Neill's ideas about Josie's physical characteristics also violate traditional and theatrical stereotypes. Through female spectacle, theatre and film create mirrors for male desire; hence, the females in these roles are expected to live up to certain physical standards. O'Neill's Josie, however, does not. She is big, overweight, and far from glamorous. Lawrence Langer, who participated in *Moon's* first production, said that the role called for

> exactly the kind of woman who, when she comes to see you and asks whether she should attempt a career in the theatre—you look embarrassed and reply, "Well, I'm afraid you're rather a big girl—how are we going to find a man tall enough to play opposite you?" (qtd. in Bogard 451–52)

For John Henry Raleigh, O'Neill creates through Josie a "wholly admirable central character" for the first time in his career ("Irish" 235). While Raleigh is not alone in viewing Josie favorably, he points to O'Neill's Irish roots as an explanation for this character. Josie is one of the

> fabled warrior women of the Celtic race. . . . Warriors, teachers of wisdom and feats of arms, eminent in their society, women in one phase of Irish mythology were assigned an especially significant role in the cult of rebirth: it was the woman, not the man, who was the spiritual vehicle who conveys the soul of the dead to rebirth in a later generation. ("Irish" 234–35)

While such a role may also be yet another version of the Madonna category of the feminine dialectic, it was a role that permitted women some qualities traditionally associated with the male role: these women had physical and spiritual power. To some extent, then, the qualities that many admire in the character of Josie Hogan are not strictly feminine but almost hermaphroditic. Even Josie's role as mother in the Hogan household is a makeshift one. By toying with conventional expectations regarding feminine beauty and behavior as well as by creating an entirely likable character, O'Neill may be assuring his audiences that questioning or violating traditional representational forms actually enhances rather than destroys our culture.

In many ways, the characterization of James Tyrone dictates the characterization of Josie. Like many of O'Neill's men, Jamie perceives women dualistically, as mothers or whores. He is, moreover, probably the most extreme example of this phenomenon in the O'Neill canon. He cannot even admit the term *wife*, a culturally sanctioned combination of mother and sexual object, into his psycholinguistic system. Because Josie is such a character, neither mother nor prostitute, but a woman who would love to love Jamie, and because his treatment of her is so abusive, he clearly cannot accept her love, or anyone else's, because he is locked into his prejudices concerning life and women. For example, he is so accustomed to associating sex with prostitutes that he cannot express his love towards Josie physically. When he tries, he immediately launches into his "prostitute behavior," even after Josie admits that she is a virgin and that she loves him. When Josie offers him her bed, he says:

> Sure thing, Kiddo. What the hell else do you suppose I came for? I've been kidding myself. (*He steps up beside her and puts his arm around her and presses his body to hers.*) You're the goods, Kid. I've wanted you all along. Love, nuts! I'll show you what love is. I know what you want, Bright Eyes. (*She [Josie] is staring at him now with a look of frightened horror. He kisses her roughly.*) Come on, Baby Doll, let's hit the hay. (925)

For Jamie, sex means the woman is a prostitute, no matter who that woman is. As the play demonstrates, it is an automatic or natural response for Jamie; he is programmed to respond to women in this manner. For Jamie, sex is perverse, a violation of the maternal ideal that he has progressively sanctified throughout *Long Day's Journey into Night* and *Moon*.

Michael Hinden argues that Tyrone's inability to have sex with Josie is a sign of transcendence. Vile, physical love is transformed into a good, holy, and pure religious experience. He notes that "Josie's early sexual interest is transcended, and for Jim she understands that she unites maternal and religious needs" (245). Josie does dismiss her desires, but as the play demonstrates, it is because Jamie can view women in no other way; his "patriarchal blindness" destroys him. Josie's desires, more importantly, are not condemned by the play; instead, O'Neill presents them sympathetically. Josie perceives Jamie's inability to see female desire and chooses to play the role of virgin for him throughout the evening, sacrificing her own desires for the sake of his. She recovers from his rough treatment and offers herself as a Madonna. Josie is not misled by the false promises of either the Madonna or the prostitute role, but for this evening anyway, she is willing to make the sacrifice, a sacrifice O'Neill accentuates through her struggles with her feelings for Jamie and with her own desire. Since Josie does not move into the role easily and since she must deny part of herself in order to play it, O'Neill makes it clear that such roles neglect to account for female desire. Josie is not a passive reflector of male desire, as Robert Heilman argues (110), but an active participant in the masquerade of gender. Through the conflict between Josie's own desire and Jamie's needs, the play illustrates that women do make sacrifices when playing these roles.

During this gender play, Jamie confesses to Josie his inability to reconcile femininity by anything but a stereotypical method. His story of his mother's corpse on the train and his sexual escapades with the "blonde pig" are an accurate image for his double vision of women. In one car, his mother is laid out in her coffin, and in another, he "lays" the whore, but neither female mirror brings him fulfillment. Like Don Parritt in *The Iceman*

Cometh, Jamie cannot build an existential illusion upon maternal turf. Because Jamie has so identified his image of himself with his mother, when he meets her at her deathbed, he sees, as he tells us in *Long Day's Journey into Night*, "the dead part of himself" (821). Since he cannot face himself as lacking, he identifies himself with the mirror, the dead female corpse. Jamie tries to take on the role of the grieving son at her funeral, but it offers nothing for him except more self-loathing. Without his mirror, Jamie is lost, a fragmented, tortured soul who cannot function. As he confesses in *Long Day's Journey into Night*, Jamie is nothing without a good woman's love. However, *Moon* demonstrates that Jamie needs not just any good woman but his mother.

Josie provides a moment of solace for Jamie, but since she is not his mother, it is only temporary. In the final moments of the third act, when Josie is almost deified, her characterization parallels that of the melodramatic heroine. As Michael Manheim notes, this scene reflects O'Neill's belief that

> the mother-infant image is to O'Neill the greatest image of life-sustaining love because it combines the physical and the emotional. If we are cut off from either, we die: physically if we don't receive the nourishment, emotionally if we don't receive the tenderness. (*Kinship* 206)

Josie, then, is the means by which Jamie attains this imaginary fulfillment.

Of course, this moment of the play fetishizes the maternal role, but it is not O'Neill's final image in the play. O'Neill does not leave us with a modern Pieta image in which a woman functions as an all-forgiving, all-sustaining mother. In the words of Samuel Beckett's wanderers in *Waiting for Godot*, Josie may give birth to herself and Jamie, but it is a birth "astride the grave." As she tells her father, a miracle has occurred: "A virgin . . . bears a dead child in the night, and the dawn finds her still a virgin" (936). The ideal female may provide nourishment, but it is transitory. In the final act, Josie and Jamie must

separate, and while Josie continues her struggle and finds a new
way of looking at herself by performing the Madonna role, Jamie
cannot reconcile his dualistic view of women and is destined to
die.

  While both the Madonna and whore roles remove women
from the world, one by elevating and the other by debasing
women, the role of a forgiving Madonna is a refreshing one.
Josie's sacrifice is acknowledged, at least, and at the end of the
play, she clearly has decided to accept herself as she is and not to
adopt the role of either whore or mother. Though remnants of
the dual categories persist, O'Neill has attempted at least to
revise these roles.

> With the greatest of difficulty she [Josie] brings herself to
> renounce the belief that with Jim she might fulfill her need
> to love and be loved. . . . To gain something new, Josie
> must renounce something old. Hers is the work of mourn-
> ing. By it she loses a ghost that haunts her, and gains a new
> sense of herself. . . . The world ceases to seem a place
> where all things are possible. It becomes one governed by
> laws of finitude, exclusion, time, place, and mortality. . . .
> In Act Four we witness evidence of Josie's growth. She now
> perceives her father from the viewpoint of another adult,
> rather than that of a dutiful and partly dependent daughter.
> (Black 544–45)

By renouncing her desire for Jamie in the third act, Josie
removes herself, as much as possible, from the manipulative
sexual economy. She is no longer entirely the object of male
desire. Her acting as the vehicle for Jamie's forgiveness, of
course, objectifies her to some extent, but once he leaves, she
begins to take some control of the stage, her household, and her
father. Josie recognizes her own power by standing up to her
father at the end of the play, and though she may never leave his
house, she will no longer be imprisoned by it. By concluding the
play in this way, O'Neill not only predicts a new theatre through
Jamie's praise of David Belasco, but he also presents a new
concept of femininity. Even though O'Neill cannot entirely

exorcise his ideals about women, he is aware that the old ways, the tendency to divide women from themselves for the sake of male desire, is detrimental to both men and women. The dawn of *Moon* brings hope; unlike Abbie in *Desire under the Elms*, Josie does not follow "her man" to his death and destiny. She remains at home, struggling to find a new way of life within the walls of the old law.

Unlike the women in *The Iceman Cometh* who haunt their men from their imprisonment behind the glass and unlike Evelyn and Mary Tyrone who have internalized the female mirror and are shattered by it, Josie consciously chooses the Madonna role. Consequently, Josie is the most fully present female character in the O'Neill canon. We see her desires, and we see them thwarted through male expectations, but we also see Josie recover, although she does not necessarily triumph. She is not Madonna, virgin, or prostitute, but instead a woman who offers a glimmer of hope to other women in the male wasteland.

3

"A Tick in the Night"
Pinter's Whores

> I've never had a whore under this roof before. Ever since your mother died.
>
> — Max in Pinter's *Homecoming*

WHILE much of the criticism of the work of Eugene O'Neill relies heavily on its autobiographical content, perhaps due to the voluminous information available, readers of Harold Pinter must rely on sparse and often enigmatic interviews. In an early statement in the program notes to *The Room* and *The Dumb Waiter* in 1960, Pinter, in one of his characteristic paradoxes, definitively states that his plays are about incomprehensibility:

> The desire for verification is understandable but cannot always be satisfied. There are no hard distinctions between what is real and what is unreal, nor between what is true and what is false. The thing is not necessarily either true or false; it can be both true and false. . . . A character on the stage who can present no convincing argument or information as to his past experience, his present behavior or his aspirations, nor give a comprehensive analysis of his motives, is as legitimate and as worthy of attention as one who, alarmingly, can do all these things. (qtd. in Esslin, *Absurd* 206)

In effect, Pinter summarizes the ideological basis for the theatre of the absurd, as well as the poststructuralists' theories concerning existence and language. The desire for stability, answers, and meaning cannot be ignored, but to presume that this desire constitutes either truth or a controllable reality is misdirected. Pinter's own reluctance to offer biographical facts may, then, reflect his own creative practices. His life, like the lives of his characters, can exist and affect audiences without extensive biographical exposition.

Lately, however, Pinter appears to be going through a creative and personal crisis. In a recent interview, he is clearly distraught over the political oppression occurring throughout the world, and he blames the United States for many of the world's problems (Kennedy 38–39). Clearly, this poet of the inarticulate, this creator of stutterers and mutes, must rethink his perception of the power of language and the human voice. He reconciles the apparent contradiction by concluding that we must continue to speak out against oppression, and he claims that all his plays prior to his more recent and clearly political pieces such as *One for the Road* and *Mountain Language* are, in fact, political (Pinter, "Play" 5–24; Merritt 213–75).

This statement has returned Pinter scholars to his earlier works. Others have dismissed Pinter's statement, arguing that he is merely going through a "second adolescence."[1] While authorial statements about literary works are often suspect, the furor Pinter has created recently is telling, for it indicates that many critics still separate art from politics. For a feminist critic, the close relationship between the two is taken for granted. Simply because women have been denied access to art, labor, and even their own bodies, all activities take on political significance: the personal is political. From a feminist perspective, then, Pinter's earlier plays are inherently political as a result of their focus on gender and domestic relations.

In terms of women, Pinter's early plays illustrate the limits of the stereotypical roles in the phallic economy. *The Room* (1957), *The Birthday Party* (1958), and *A Slight Ache* (1961) all present mothers with sexual desire in some form or another, and this addition is unsettling for both the male characters and their audiences. However, *The Homecoming* (1965), one of the classics of modern drama, is particularly problematic and has provoked voluminous critical responses that try to place Ruth in either the prostitute or Madonna category.[2] Because of this disagreement, as well as Pinter's twenty-five-year defense of Ruth, I will begin my analysis of Pinter's women with this play (qtd. in Halton 194–95; Hewes 56; Gussow 17). In *The Homecoming*, as well as other plays, Pinter does not categorize women stereotypically. In fact, like O'Neill, he exposes the patriarchal process of female objectification.

Pinter's personal relationships with women are not as well documented as O'Neill's. Born in 1930, Pinter was separated from his mother and father during World War II, but there is little evidence to suggest that this separation affected him as dramatically as O'Neill's mother's morphine addiction haunted and inspired his works. After working in the theatre as an actor in small parts, Pinter met Vivien Merchant, and they were married in 1956. Together they worked in theatres across London, and as Pinter began writing, Merchant performed as Pinter's onstage women "largely because she so perfectly embodied the self-possessed sex bomb ticking at the center of Pinter's onstage ménages" (Schiff 301). After nineteen years of marriage, however, Pinter began an affair with Lady Antonia Fraser, a writer, historian, and member of Britain's ruling class. Merchant and some critics of Pinter's work took the separation very hard, and its announcement created "one of the biggest press bonfires of the British seventies" (Schiff 301). Merchant finally and reluctantly granted Pinter a divorce in the late seventies after fighting the divorce, refusing to sign the papers, and creating a media field day. Fraser and Pinter were married in 1980, and Merchant died in 1982 of "chronic alcoholism" (Schiff 302).

This information, of course, can be used to both support and attack Pinter. For sympathetic readers, Pinter's second marriage marks a narrow escape from a jealous, possessive woman. For his detractors, the event illustrates Pinter's misogyny. Because of the limited biographical material available, such judgments seem premature, and even if they are true,

Pinter does not appear to be tortured concerning questions of femininity or female love objects in the way that O'Neill was. Part of the reason for this may be the cultural context that Pinter inhabits. While far from reaching its goals or being accepted completely in either Britain or the United States, feminism does exist in Western culture. During O'Neill's era, feminist ideals were new, and everyone concerned struggled with their implications. Though it is certainly true today, feminism during the seventies took a radical turn: women not only wanted access to the workplace, but they also argued for benefits within the home. Moreover, women had proved themselves entirely capable of doing men's work during World War II. The problem was retaining the gains made during the war and struggling against the culture's attempt to return them to the home. The women's movement of O'Neill's day argued for modified roles, whereas the more contemporary feminism of Pinter's day "is based on a rejection of traditional roles in favor of equality, and it demands a broad-based agenda of changes in the fundamental arrangement of home and work" (Klein 82).

Pinter's own experiments in language, roles, and characterization run against the grain of female stereotyping, or any stereotyping for that matter. His different vision is clearly reflected in his plays' structures and forms, a technique that has baffled critics and prompted many to identify his work as some composite or mixture of absurdism, naturalism, and realism.[3] In addition, Pinter's use of language is similar to the ways many poststructuralists, including Lacan and Irigaray, view language. Like these theorists, Pinter seeks to expose the gaps in communication rather than reconstructing the rigid linguistic structure that many have identified as patriarchal or phallocentric (Sarbin 34). In Pinter's works, language often does not communicate clearly; subtext and the "play of signification" are in fact what make his plays so difficult to explicate. There is not just one meaning but instead, a number of meanings, a play of voices from not just a number of characters, as in O'Neill, but from an individual character.

> Through the atypical qualities of his plays, Pinter tries to
> keep us disoriented so that we can remain aware of our own
> mental and emotional processes, of our involvement in the
> play and its making. This preoccupation of Pinter's reflects
> his deep interest, not only in *The Dumb Waiter* but else-
> where, in the question of how events, in drama and life, are
> defined. (Van Laan 501)

Though Pinter did not always use this technique in con-
junction with gender, his later plays align this technique with
central female characters in domestic settings. Early in his
career, for example, Kenneth Tynan asks Pinter why he does not
write about sex in his plays (qtd. in Esslin, *Pinter* 38). However,
by combining in these later works the method of the absurd with
the domestic setting and its issues, Pinter creates dramas that
not only address the universal condition of modern existence
but also the condition of females in this culture. Though his
plays address ubiquitous issues, they should not overshadow
Pinter's unique and disturbing representation of female characters. Like O'Neill, Pinter dismantles the gender ideology that
forces women to inhabit a "kind of Alaska," a marginalized
position that denies female desire and female voices. This is not
to imply that the female characters in Pinter's plays do not have
access to language or that they create a language of their own,
but rather that through their behavior and their manipulation of
language, they create a "stir" among their audiences and male
counterparts. In this way, even in the plays in which women do
not appear onstage, they function as whores, women who express their desire, a desire that has been denied by the phallic
economy and that threatens to expose the fact that this means of
oppression is done with mirrors—a cheap magic trick.

Pinter's own response to his mirror image illustrates the
difference between his representation of women and O'Neill's.
During an interview with Lawrence Bensky, Pinter states: "I
had—I have—nothing to say about myself, directly. I wouldn't
know where to begin. Particularly since I often look at myself in
the mirror and say, 'Who the hell's that?'" ("Interview" 20).

Unlike O'Neill, who uses the mirror to confirm his sense of identity or existence, the mirror for Pinter confirms his own lack or inadequacy. In Lacanian terms, such a revelation for the male subject is rare but accurate. The mirror image and all the objects that function like the mirror do not accurately reflect. In the above statement and in his plays, Pinter indicates that he sees both subjectivity and the means by which it is constructed in a more complex, unconventional way than O'Neill does.

The Homecoming

The Homecoming (1965) has perhaps attracted more critical attention than any other Pinter play, and the character who has generated the most discussion is Ruth. Scholars and critics are particularly concerned about Ruth's decision to leave her respectable American existence as housewife, mother, and editor in order to live with her husband's family, a group of men who offer her a life of prostitution. While much of the early criticism of the play does not explicitly condemn Pinter's work for violating the mutually exclusive roles of Madonna and prostitute, the implication is there. Ruth, after all, forgoes her duties as a wife and mother in order to remain in a household of men of questionable character.

> If a work is pornographic because it toys with the most easily manipulated human emotions—those of sex and (more especially) violence—without pausing to relate cause and effect, then The Homecoming can even be said to fall into such a category. (Trussler 134)

Martin Esslin's attempts to rescue the play and Ruth from the realm of the pornographic in many ways does more harm than good. He concludes that Ruth is a prostitute masquerading as a Madonna, so her choice to remain with the men is natural. Her previous career, argues Esslin, as a "model for the body" is "widely known as a euphemism for a prostitute" (Pinter 156). The play, however, offers no indications for this conclusion. However, Ruth's sexuality and her confident expressions of female desire are easily dismissed as prostitute-like behavior, a traditional strategy for accounting for and legislating female desire within patriarchy.

It is encouraging to note that the criticism of this female character has drastically changed over the past twenty-five years, perhaps reflecting the changes and effectiveness of the women's movement. For example, Austin Quigley's reading of Ruth in 1975 could be taken from Betty Friedan's *Feminine Mystique*. In this important feminist book, Friedan illustrates the growing unrest of many American women at the time. Like Irigaray and Lacan, she indicates that this unrest, stemming from thwarted female desire, cannot find expression in the conventional forms imposed upon and available to women within patriarchy. Friedan describes it as the "the problem that has no name," a description that accurately illustrates the complicity of the linguistic system in the social, emotional, and economic oppression of women.

> If I am right, the problem that has no name stirring in the minds of so many American women today is not a matter of loss of femininity or too much education, or the demands of domesticity. It is far more important than anyone recognizes. . . . It may well be the key to our future as a nation and a culture. We can no longer ignore that voice within women that says: "I want something more than my husband and my children and my home." (Friedan 27)

For Quigley and many feminists of this era and today, this "something more" is a career; Ruth's behavior is the result of her frustrations about being a housewife (*Pinter* 218).

More recent criticism reflects a radical feminism that argues that Ruth overturns the traditional patriarchal hierarchy. She gains control over the men who have tried to control her.[4] While this inversion takes place throughout the play, such an inversion does not change the phallocentric hierarchy. Whether a man is in power or a woman, the need for an oppressed term remains. For Elizabeth Sakellaridou, Ruth's manipulation merely mimics male power throughout the play (119).

Admittedly, Ruth uses both inversion and mimicry in order to fulfill her female desire, and through these strategies, the play illustrates the limitations of female stereotypes. Ruth is "outside traditional boundaries by the failure of such conventions such as marriage" (Gale 154). What is so interesting about the play, however, is Ruth's decision to remain with the men at the end of the play. For those who argue for the inversion approach, this decision reflects the phallocentric need for an oppressed term in order to ascend to power. But Ruth mimics and inverts patriarchal systems so as to create a space for her feminine difference and desire without dismissing heterosexual relations altogether. The play does not create a pristine feminist space above and beyond the patriarchal fray, nor does it objectify a woman within such a system. In this way, Pinter creates a complex and subtle approach to feminism and female power that accounts for heterosexual relations.

Through the use of the domestic setting in *The Homecoming*, Pinter establishes audience expectations in a fashion similar to O'Neill: the home is a lure, a line that promises but does not deliver the nurturing ideals society expects from this social institution.

> In spite of the clever dislocation of common sense, Pinter's plays affect us because they are about the middle-class family, both as sheltering home longed for and dreamed of, and as many-tentacled monster strangling its victim. It does not, after all, surprise us that there is more menace and irrationality in this dramatic material than in any other. (Storch 136)

Given the conflicting readings of Ruth, however, Pinter clearly surprises many of his readers. Unlike Brecht who advocated unusual settings in order to dislocate the audience (190–91), Pinter and O'Neill use the familiar in unfamiliar ways in order to disrupt their audiences. By choosing the traditional setting of the home, Pinter and O'Neill encourage us to revise our views of such dramatic settings, forms, and social institutions. Unexpected action is framed by the traditional in order not only that we may see the form in a new way, but also that we may view such a form more critically in the future.

The setting also highlights the patriarchal nature of the surroundings: "It's a sterile world from which women have been excluded; the set has to mirror that" (Hall 11). As Teddy tells Ruth: "Actually there was a wall, across there . . . with a door. We knocked it down . . . years ago . . . to make an open living area. The structure wasn't affected, you see. My mother was dead" (21). The simultaneous elimination of the mother and the wall indicates that the men have attempted to eliminate gender division from the household as well. Without the wall and without Jessie, there is no disruptive feminine presence, no anxiety of castration. Through this attempt to repress the mother and the feminine, however, they have in effect created another "hole," a symbolic reminder of castration.

By postponing Ruth's arrival, however, Pinter has the opportunity to establish a world without women and, through the interchanges among Lenny, Max, Sam, and Joey, to give the reader a sense of the manner in which it functions. Like O'Neill's male characters in *The Iceman Cometh*, Pinter's men struggle to uphold their illusions of autonomy. But unlike the O'Neill play, Pinter's play demonstrates that the strategies by which these illusions are upheld are constantly changing. Further, unlike the men in Harry Hope's saloon, Pinter's male characters do not judiciously adhere to the pipe dreams of their comrades, periodically mirroring one another's image. Pinter's men abuse each other mercilessly. Each attempts symbolically to castrate the other males in the house in order to create an oppressed term by which they can gain a sense of autonomy. Here, violence and verbal abuse, not the etiquette of O'Neill's pipe dreams, construct the existential mirror.

The play quickly establishes this method of interaction in the opening scene. While Lenny reads the paper, Max and he exchange barbs. In addition, the scene establishes a dialectic between experiential knowledge and learned knowledge, "hands-on" activities and those imagined or fictional. In this way, *The Homecoming*, like O'Neill's *Iceman Cometh*, explores the relationship between illusion and reality. As the play progresses, however, it becomes clear that Pinter is not examining the relationship in the same way as O'Neill. The men tell tall tales continually. It is difficult to know whether these narratives are real or imagined, and to some extent, it does not matter.

The opening scene also establishes the manner by which the men in the house respond to absent females. Lenny, for example, only reads about the horses in the paper, while Max has "held them" and "calmed them down before a big race," particularly the fillies that he mesmerized and calmed by his look alone (10). Max insists that he can control women and the memory of them, while Lenny cannot.

This emphasis on sight is important to both Pinter's play and psychoanalytic theory because it presumes male mastery via the optical alone. The male spectator has the power to control the female object. This optical ability is consistent with Freud's, Lacan's, and Irigaray's theories on patriarchy. As Freud makes clear, the sight of the female genitals—the lack of the penis—initiates the castration complex, and later establishes male domination. Irigaray explains that prior to this event, the little girl believes that

> *she had, in her clitoris, a significant phallic organ. . . .*
> But the sight of the penis—and this is the inverse of what happens to the little boy discovering his sister's genitals—shows the little girl to what extent her clitoris is unworthy of comparison to the boy's sex organ. She understands, finally, the prejudice—the anatomical prejudice—that is her fate, and forces herself to accept castration, not as the threat of a loss, the fear of a not yet accomplished act, but as a *fait accompli*: an amputation already performed. (*This Sex* 39)

For Laura Mulvey, the spectacle of woman in traditional Hollywood cinema replays this moment perpetually, giving the male viewers a sense of power and the females a sense of lack or inferiority (14–25). Lacan and others refer to this process as the *look*, that which objectifies and gives the seeing male subject a sense of mastery. Throughout the Pinter play, Max and others use their look, as well as their control of memories and narratives in order to objectify female counterparts.

Max's first memory of his wife, Jessie, makes it clear that his memories of Jessie may change at breakneck speed, but they are all created in order to bolster his own sense of identity. In the opening scene, for example, he describes Jessie as follows: "Mind you, she wasn't such a bad woman. Even though it made me sick just to look at her rotten stinking face, she wasn't a bad bitch. I gave her the best bleeding years of my life anyway" (9). Lacan argues that men frequently grow tired of their women, their love objects, but rather than examining their own need for these objects in their lives, men frequently move on to other women. Pinter's play highlights the fickleness of masculine desire through Max's description of Jessie that oscillates to such an extreme that her description shifts from an ordinary wife to a "stinking whore." As Louise Kaplan notes, however, such changing attitudes characterize the patriarchy's perception of women. Citing Shakespeare's *King Lear*, Kaplan notes:

> Lear's portrayal of the female as a creature divided at the waist with angelic breasts above and fiendish genitals below is a common enough female stereotype. . . . Lear was not the first nor will he be the last to entertain the fantasy. (43)

While Max is not as anatomically specific as Lear, his memories of his wife change from Madonna to whore throughout the play, depending on his own desires.

More importantly, in this household of men, Max, who claims that he has suffered the pain of childbirth, frequently plays the role of the female.

> In this role Max oscillates between emotional security and vulnerability. On the one hand he boasts of the primacy of man's abilities as a homemaker, but on the other, he mani-

fests a recurring need to justify himself in terms of achieve-
ments in the world outside the home. (Quigley, *Pinter* 180)

Max's oscillation from male to female roles not only violates
conventions of the well-made play that posits unified and consistent character development, but such oscillation also indicates
that he uses such roles to gain power, to uphold his illusions
about himself, not the illusions of the other males in the family.
In this way, Pinter exposes the patriarchal use of femininity: it is
another existential act, a performance that brings about male
fulfillment. As Max tells Joey after he has violently punched
Joey, "What you've got to do is you've got to learn how to defend
yourself, and you've got to learn how to attack" (17).

Max, of course, knows the rules well. For example, when
he feels threatened by the accomplishments of his brother Sam
outside the home, Max makes it clear that he carries a big stick:
"It's funny you never got married, isn't it? A man with all your
gifts" (14). When he tries to impress Ruth later in the play, he
says that he was both mother and father to his sons, a complete
parent. While Max may play a woman, play a lack, he is usually
in control of these roles. He quickly dissociates himself from
either male or female categories depending on the context and
on whether he is attacking or defending. Unlike many female
characters who have such roles imposed on them, as the patriarch of this family, Max believes he has access to all roles, no
matter how contradictory, and he uses them all to establish his
power in the male household.

However, Lenny sees through Max's game and insults him
in both of his roles. In the first scene, for example, he first
deactivates Max as a man by labeling him as the female support
for the family, and then he discounts Max's ability to even play
that role by telling him he is a bad cook. Lenny bolsters his
power further by playing the role of a frightened little boy: "Oh,
Daddy, you're not going to use your stick on me, are you? Eh?
Don't use your stick on me Daddy" (11). Because Lenny has in
effect castrated Max, it is unlikely that his fear is genuine; it,

too, is a performance. At the same time, however, Lenny's performance may force Max to confront the reality of his assumed or constructed power.

Performances, narratives, and memories are all used to win the power game in this masculine household. The man who tells the best story, throws the best punch, or has the best memory, gains momentary control. And while Max functions as a surrogate mother for the family, he will not let his sons or Ruth forget that he is, first of all, a man, also trying to win at the game in this London household. However, Pinter symbolically undercuts Max's aspirations to power by depicting him as a man with a withered stick.

With the arrival of Ruth, the play relentlessly exposes the illusions the men foster in this male wasteland. Ruth does not simply take control, but she shatters the glass of female objectification more completely than any character I have discussed thus far. She functions as a "tick in the night," causing trouble in the commonplace phallic economy. As Lenny says:

> I mean there are lots of things which tick in the night, don't you find that? All sorts of objects, which, in the day, you wouldn't call anything else but commonplace. They give you no trouble. But in the night any given one of a number of them is liable to start letting out a bit of tick. (28)

Perhaps aware of the threat Ruth poses, Lenny attempts to intimidate Ruth through one of his numerous "whore-or" stories, a narrative in which he violently assaults a "diseased whore." Ruth responds to this performance by asking, "How did you know she was diseased?" (31).

With a commonplace query, Ruth castrates Lenny. She effectively cuts his tale short. It is also important to note that Ruth does not accuse Lenny of lying. She does not invert the patriarchal hierarchy by establishing her position as the subject supposed to know. Instead, she forces Lenny to expose his imaginary status, his role as tale-teller, a creator of male fantasies.

Lenny's response, "I decided she was" (31), is important, for throughout the play, women both onstage and off, are frequently described as diseased. Rolf Fjelde, for example, notes that the reason for Jessie's absence as a mother is that she, like Max's own mother, was diseased. Her inability to play simply Madonna or prostitute roles transforms her into a "diseased whore":

> Since Jessie *is* absent, and her exposition is made both meager and ambiguous, we can never know exactly what her character was, except that the contagion spreads—in all but Joey, the only one who neither shares nor needs the ritual cigar—from her dual and unreconcilable roles of the good wife and mother and the deceiving slutbitch. (102)

However, Fjelde does not take into account the context of Max's comments about Jessie. Max tells this story while Ruth and the rest of the family listen. Once again, he performs in order to construct another, more sympathetic version of his identity. More importantly, this opening scene between Ruth and Lenny should alert us to the men's tendency to control women by labeling them "diseased." When women do not cooperate or fulfill their desires, the men in this play conclude that there is something wrong, something unnatural about the women.

The "kind of Alaska" Ruth has previously inhabited is clearly illustrated by her and Teddy's descriptions of her American existence. While Teddy praises her as a dutiful wife and mother, Ruth condemns her existence and the country as a wasteland, "all rock. And sand" (53). As Ruth demonstrates and as Teddy's repeated references to her illness indicate, Ruth has grown dissatisfied with this role, so Teddy, too, concludes that there is something wrong with her.

During her interactions with Lenny, it is as if Ruth is preparing herself for her later battle with Teddy. During Lenny's second "whore-or" story, Ruth continues to challenge Lenny on linguistic grounds by calling him by his birth name.

Ruth's final masterstroke—think-acting her way into the one unassailable position—is to call Lenny "Leonard," as

his dead mother used to, thereby asserting her dominance
on the most immediate level and at the same time setting up
resonances which continue to vibrate in the memory all
through the play. (Taylor 65)

From a feminist perspective, Ruth's behavior is even more
revolutionary. By calling Lenny by the name his mother used,
Ruth aligns herself with the matriarchal, not the patriarchal.
She, a woman, gives Lenny a name, an action that violates the
Western tradition of men naming women when heterosexual
relationships are established through marriage.

At this early stage in the play, Ruth inverts the patriarchal
system by taking on the role of the man. From a dominant
position, she offers to pour water down Lenny's throat; it is she,
not the man, who possesses the life fluid. When she drains the
glass herself, Ruth underscores her power. She will fulfill herself. She will not mirror male desires, for she leaves behind an
empty glass. Because Lenny drains his own glass once Ruth has
gone, the play seems to hint at the possibility of some sort of
heterosexual relationship and sense of identity for both men and
women that does not require the objectification of women. As
Katherine Burkman argues, with Ruth's

> exultant draining of the glass of water, Ruth asserts her own
> full-bodied sexuality in the face of his impotence, although
> Lenny's draining of his own glass of water after she exits
> suggests the possibility of his redemption through Ruth
> from that condition. (*Godot* 134)

Such a reading is supported by several incidents that occur
later in the play. Ruth's behavior during the philosophical
discussion between Lenny and Teddy is particularly noteworthy. At first, Ruth sits by quietly, but then she interrupts by
focusing the men's attention on the body, not the mind:

> You've forgotten something. Look at me. I . . . move my
> leg. That's all it is. But I wear . . . underwear . . . which
> moves with me . . . it captures your attention. Perhaps you
> misinterpret. The action is simple. It's a leg . . . moving.

My lips move. Why don't you restrict . . . your observa-
tions to that? Perhaps the fact that they move is more
significant . . . than the words which come through them.
You must bear that . . . possibility . . . in mind. (52–53)

In this sexually charged speech, Ruth begins by courting the
male look, the optical means of female objectification, but just
as she courts it, she also disrupts it, creating what Lacan calls
the "gaze." "If the eye is that which sees, the gaze is that which
elides the eye and shows us how we are caught out by our own
look—displaced in the act of spectatorship" (Freedman 1). The
eye of the object also looks, captures, and objectifies.

Ruth, moreover, reminds the men that her legs and lips
move, and while she does not explicitly refer to female genitalia,
the association is there. Such a reminder threatens the men in
the play because it reminds them of her female sexuality that
does not require male intervention. As Irigaray argues, female
genitalia are constantly touching. Woman

> finds pleasure almost anywhere. Even if we refrain from
> invoking the hystericization of her entire body, the geogra-
> phy of her pleasure is far more diversified, more multiple in
> its differences, more complex, more subtle, than is com-
> monly imagined—in an imaginary rather too narrowly fo-
> cused on sameness. (*This Sex* 28)

Simply put, Ruth's response reminds her male counterparts that
they and their look do not see or perceive the entire picture.
They are missing something, lacking.

Rather than dismissing Ruth as diseased, however the play
illustrates that Ruth's behavior has significantly affected many of
the men. When Lenny and Joey, for example, attempt to tell yet
another "whore-or" story in which women are humiliated, their
narrative is disjointed and cut short. Ruth has disrupted their
linguistic mastery. And when Lenny and Ruth are together at
the end of the play, Lenny says that he purchased a hat for one of
his female friends, after he learns that Ruth was a model.
Instead of another sadistic, slut story, Lenny presents a narra-

tive in which he demonstrated affection toward another woman. Joey, too, says, "Sometimes . . . you can be happy . . . and not go the whole hog" (68). There is a middle ground.

> As Ruth exits under the arch that commemorates the con-
> clusion of Jessie's control of the family, she does so with a
> new female control. . . . In her efforts to establish that
> control, she has exhibited characteristics that make it clear
> that she, like Lenny, is not circumscribed by the roles
> assigned to her in the family structure to which she cur-
> rently belongs. (Quigley, *Pinter* 197)

That Ruth gains control and power in this household is clear, but she is not entirely divorced from the household. While Lenny, for example, can no longer tell his abusive narra-tives, Ruth, too, has been affected by her interactions with Lenny. In an early speech, Lenny admits that he has always imagined himself as a soldier in Venice during the Italian campaign in World War II (30). When Teddy confronts Ruth about her decision to leave him and remain with his family, he reminds her of Venice in order to encourage her to stay with him. However, she uses Lenny's imaginary narrative saying, "But if I'd been a nurse in the Italian campaign I would have been there before" (55). Through this small detail, the play indicates that Ruth has not entirely removed herself from the men in the play. There is some collaboration possible. Ruth is not above and beyond the men in the role of either Madonna or termagant. She is with them, establishing her power within a patriarchal system. Admittedly, the men towards the end of the play misread Ruth's expression of feminine difference. They view her as a prostitute. Here, too, though, Ruth makes her desires known, manipulating the men through their desires by requesting more than they had presumed she would require.

Teddy is one of the only men in the house who does not participate in or appreciate the female difference. When the entire family turns to Ruth, tries to touch and understand her, Teddy renounces them and declares his position as the controlling subject supposed to know, the possessor of the look, not the gaze: "You're just objects. You just . . . move about. I can observe it. I can see what you do. It's the same as I do. But you're lost in it. You won't get me being . . . I won't be lost in it" (62).

Sam, whom Teddy claims he has always had a great affinity for, is also reluctant to participate. He blurts out the truth about Jessie—she had an adulterous affair—but the rest of the men in the family take no notice. Such revelations have no significance; Sam's prostrate body remains on the floor, a remnant of the phallic economy that views female sexuality and desire as a life-threatening event.

The play concludes with a Pinteresque Pieta. The men surround Ruth, the woman who may turn to prostitution, the woman who left her family, husband, and children, the woman who violates the stereotypes of the phallic economy. By concluding the play in this way, Pinter does not create yet another idealized space for femininity. Ruth does not become a Madonna or prostitute. Having challenged the objectification of the look, as well as the traditional categories assigned to women, the image remains enigmatic in order to account for feminine difference. Jessie and Ruth both turn "male categories against men" (Postlewait 210). By playing the prostitute, Ruth becomes a whore, which affords female desire and which the play honors through this final image. Throughout the play, Ruth has successfully shattered her "kind of Alaska." As Max says, she may not be "adaptable." But because she remains with the men, the play indicates that some relation that does not require female objectification is possible within the phallic economy.

No Man's Land

Frequently compared to the work of Samuel Beckett and T. S. Eliot, No Man's Land (1975) illustrates the desolate nature of modern, human existence. Furthermore, since no women appear onstage, it is tempting to ignore this play in terms of questions regarding gender and to conclude that Pinter's play

explores themes that apply to the human condition in general.
From a feminist perspective, such conclusions are suspect. In
her study of American fiction, Judith Fetterley, who is a feminist
but not a psychoanalytic critic, warns feminist critics about
universal themes. Like Irigaray, she argues that within the
phallic economy *universal* generally indicates *male* (xi–xii).
Elizabeth Sakellaridou, who devotes an entire book to the study
of Pinter's female characters and who argues that Pinter slowly
comes to an understanding of female representation as his
creative work progresses, notes that this and his other all-male
plays forestall what she sees as his "endeavour to present the
male and female principles on equal terms" (120).

While I do not agree with Sakellaridou's conclusion, her
point raises an interesting question about Pinter's decision to
create *No Man's Land*. Martin Esslin implies that the play relies
on the techniques that defined Pinter's earlier works: "As in so
many of Pinter's earlier plays, we experience the terror aroused
by the appearance of a new and mysterious character," Spooner
in this case (*Pinter* 199). In terms of gender, too, Pinter seems to
be regressing, or in Elizabeth Sakellaridou's words, "trying to
shake off a deeply felt feminine influence" (11). In *The Homecoming*, Pinter creates a complex female character. And in the
full-length play that immediately preceded *No Man's Land*, *Old
Times* (1971), Pinter not only creates an interesting female
character but also dramatizes the threat a female friendship
poses for the male character, Deeley, in the play. Pinter's
defense of this play and the female relationship in it against
attacks and productions that equated female friendship with
lesbianism are also important.

> Pinter's angry objections to Visconti's production of *Old
> Times* in Rome would suggest that, in his own view, Kate's
> and Anna's relationship cannot be accurately portrayed as
> *overtly* sexual. . . . If close friendship between women is
> threatening to men (as Kate's and Anna's past friendship
> is/was to Deeley in the play), to present it on stage as
> overtly sexual or to label it in criticism as lesbian may be a

way to deny its legitimacy by denying its normalcy. (Merritt 206)

These details suggest that far from fleeing the feminine influence in his life, Pinter may be protecting and honoring it. As many feminists are aware, the term *lesbian* is often used as a threat or a means of controlling unacceptable female behavior; that is, the term is frequently used derisively and applied to women who are not behaving according to patriarchal expectations regardless of their sexual orientation. While Pinter's reaction may indicate that he, too, views the term derisively and must defend his female characters from such an imputation, it may also indicate that he is attempting to salvage and honor this female-female relationship from partiarchal condemnation. Given his subtle and complex representations of women, Pinter's decision to return to an all-male cast in *No Man's Land* does seem surprising.

However, the play does make explicit many of the issues regarding gender that were left implied in the earlier plays. For example, the relationship between language and gender is given center stage in *No Man's Land*. The men in the play are virtually deadened by their inability to engage with women without objectifying them. Their inability takes on greater significance, since the play is set in the home of a member of Britain's ruling class. As Foster reminds Spooner:

> It's a world of silk. It's a world of organdie. It's a world of flower arrangements. It's a world of eighteenth century cookery books. It's nothing to do with toffeeapples and a packet of crisps. It's milk in the bath. It's the cloth bellpull. It's organisation. (111)

For those readers who are tempted to dismiss Pinter's characterizations by arguing that his casts are filled with the dregs of society, *No Man's Land* illustrates that his character types and the situations he draws also occur among the wealthy, educated, and politically powerful.

The similarities between *No Man's Land* and O'Neill's *Iceman Cometh* are striking. The only difference is the opulent

setting. A bar is at the center of the set, and as the play opens, a
Hickey-like character, Spooner, has just arrived. And like Hickey, he has the uncanny ability to spot pipe dreams:

> I was about to say, you see, that there are some people who
> appear to be strong, whose idea of what strength consists of
> is persuasive, but who inhabit the idea and not the fact.
> What they possess is not strength but expertise. They have
> nurtured and maintain what is in fact a calculated posture.
> Half the time it works. It takes a man of intelligence and
> perception to stick a needle through that posture and
> discern the essential flabbiness of the stance. I am such a
> man. (78)

Unlike the O'Neill play, however, the pipe dreams do not even
appear to offer the illusion of life. The character most desperately attached to his illusions, Hirst, has a name which sounds
"very much like hearse" (Gabbard 261). The exchanges between
Spooner and Hirst, moreover, indicate that the illusions Hirst
has been fostering are killing him, and at the heart of these
illusions lies an extremely ambivalent relationship towards
women.

Initially, Hirst behaves much like Teddy in Pinter's *Homecoming*. He merely watches Spooner perform; he "won't be lost
in it" (*Homecoming* 62). Gradually, however, Spooner engages
Hirst in conversation. He reminisces about a past in which male
virgins were garlanded, a time when male bonding was not only
condoned but praised. Subtly perceiving some difficulty with
Hirst's relationship to women, Spooner imaginatively creates a
wife for his host. Hirst detaches himself from this narrative by
indicating that Spooner's creation has been given legs only to
run away.

Spooner, however, will not let go and persists in challenging Hirst's relationship with this offstage, imaginary wife:

> Was she ever there? Was she ever there, in your cottage? It
> is my duty to tell you you have failed to convince. . . . I
> begin to wonder whether truly accurate and therefore

essentially poetic definition means anything to you at all. I begin to wonder whether you do in fact love her, truly caressed her, truly did cradle her, truly did husband her, falsely dreamed or did truly adore her. I have seriously questioned these propositions and find them threadbare. (93)

Hirst, who is in "the last lap of a race" he has "long forgotten to run" (94), is clearly shaken and moments after this discussion, he literally crawls out of the room.

More importantly, however, the scene explicitly aligns the concept of femininity to language and literary production. In this case, Spooner equates feminine contact with poetic definition. Further, though Spooner borders on creating some idealized view of this imaginary woman, a Muse or Madonna, his portrayal is also strangely commonplace, suggesting a meeting of minds of and bodies that creates poetic language, a language of life, not Hirst's deathly, static "no man's land." Hirst's vision of the world is clearly threatened. The concept of feminine sexuality overcomes him; he must leave the room.

When Hirst returns, he is still clearly shaken and admits that he dreamed that he was drowning. To calm himself and regain control, he seeks solace from the look and the spectacle of women in his photo album:

> The sun shone. The girls had lovely hair, dark, sometimes red. Under their dresses their bodies were white. It's all in my album. I'll find it. You'll be struck by the charm of the girls, their grace, the ease with which they sit, pour tea, loll. It's in my album. (106)

This treatment of femininity is more degrading than "Spooner's malevolent mother; his adulterous wife; and Foster's Siamese whores" (Diamond 196). Here the women are completely objectified, pressed into place, and available at all times for Hirst's voyeuristic pleasures and desire for mastery. The album is also offered to Spooner as proof of his "way with women," his sexual prowess, and patriarchal power. But as Briggs says later, "They're

blank, mate, blank. The blank dead" (137). Hirst has clearly
constructed his fantasies on feminine nothingness.

Later, Hirst's ambivalence towards women becomes more
explicit:

> There's a gap in me. I can't fill it. There's a flood running
> through me. I can't plug it. They're blotting me out. Who is
> doing it? I'm suffocating. It's a muff. A muff, perfumed.
> Someone is doing me to death. (108)

Hirst's castration fears are closely aligned with the feminine
presence. In this dream, the feminine presence paradoxically
accentuates Hirst's lack.

To combat his fear, Hirst invokes decorum, cultural stereotypes, his album, and narratives that illustrate his sexual prowess (108–27). However, Spooner attempts to break through such
defenses by continually challenging Hirst's attempts to control
women through his narrative and offers an alternative to female
objectification that would still offer Hirst a sense of mastery:

> Your face is so seldom seen, your words, known to so many,
> have been so seldom heard, in the absolute authority of
> your own rendering, that this event would qualify for that
> rarest of categories: the unique. I beg you to consider
> seriously the social implications of such an adventure. You
> would be there in body. It would bring the young to you. (148)

The homosexual implications are clear in this speech, and it
would be easy to conclude that Spooner, who has offered himself
as a "warrior" servant, will procure young men for the aging
Hirst through this public reading. But as Spooner notes, women
would attend, and he even refers to the reading by the feminine
pronoun "her" (149). Spooner is apparently offering Hirst an
alternative to his current homosocial relations but using those
relations to move Hirst beyond them. Initially, Spooner creates
an image of this event in which Hirst would play the role of
subject supposed to know, the master or "author-ity." It is a role
that Hirst is familiar with and that has characterized his position
throughout the play. Once again, however, Spooner offers a

variation on this strategy, not a new form, but one that would afford community, a variation that Spooner aligns with the feminine. Spooner's alternative highlights that it is not the inherent nature of the words Hirst uses that causes the stasis but the manner in which he controls those words. The salvation Spooner offers is the experience of what he sees as a "feminine" use of those words, one which is dynamic and communal, not like the static exclusivity of Hirst's past performances.

Hirst, however, cannot accept this alternative, so he decides to change the subject for the last time (151). Hirst cannot face either linguistic indeterminacy or the feminine. Ironically, Hirst's attempts to control and establish meaning are meaningless. More importantly, his attempts to control and objectify women lead finally to his own destruction, to a masculine wasteland in which everything remains the same, and the subject, in both senses of the word, never changes.

Betrayal

In *Betrayal* (1978), the centrality and importance of Pinter's female character, Emma, has been well documented, particularly by Katherine Burkman and Linda Ben-Zvi. While using different approaches, both critics note that Emma has been objectified by her male counterparts, and both conclude that the play documents Emma's change from an object, a dutiful wife and lover, to a woman who both understands and defies objectification. Interestingly, Pinter chooses to depict this female or feminist awakening through an antichronological structure. In *The Modern Stage and Other Worlds*, Austin Quigley extensively discusses the play's deviations from the conventions of the well-made play, which presumes coherence in the characterization and the dramatic action, but he does not align the change in dramatic form with the changing representations of Emma throughout the play.

For Enoch Brater, Pinter's decision to structure the play in an antichronological manner is inspired by his cinematic experi-

ence. The discrete scenes, the "flashbacks," and so on, all reflect
Pinter's indebtedness to film. What Pinter does not borrow from
traditional cinema, however, is the representation of women as
spectacle, objects of the masculine look. As a matter of fact,
Pinter seems determined to undermine this look on the part of
both the audience and the male characters in the play. As Alan
Varley argues, the position of spectator in this play is both
"perilous and privileged" (96).

As mentioned earlier, Jacques Derrida, Jacques Lacan,
Luce Irigaray, and others argue that phallocentrism is characterized by its rigidity, closure, oppression, and stasis, characteristics that are also used to define linguistic and philosophical
mastery; that is, phallocentrism defines such characteristics as
essential to truthful or correct discourse and thought. These
poststructuralists compellingly illustrate that even the most
flawless examples of such discourse have gaps, contradictions,
and linguistic play. These theorists do not propose that we
create another language, but instead suggest that we value the
other language that already exists in our own. To assume that
closure is possible or to attempt to define linguistic play as faulty
ignores the realities of our language. They argue for a discourse
and an ideology that would appreciate such dynamism. Further,
these theorists frequently associate the concept of play with the
feminine, yet another oppressed term in the patriarchal ideology. For example, Luce Irigaray, argues for a discourse that
would appreciate difference and avoid sameness:

> If we keep on speaking the same language together, we're
> going to reproduce the same history. . . . Listen: all round
> us, men and women sound just the same. The same discus-
> sions, the same arguments, the same scenes. (*This Sex* 205)

However, such statements have often been attacked on the
grounds that they are essentialist.

While I do not propose to argue that there is a unique
female language, though there is growing evidence that men
and women use language differently, I would like to illustrate

that in *Betrayal*, as in some other Pinter plays, gender and language are inextricably linked in order to illustrate the static and deadly nature of phallocentrism.

Emma, the main female character in *Betrayal*, for example, reads differently than her male counterparts. In a "nicely self-reflexive moment" in the play (Burkman, "Betrayal" 505), Emma's husband, Robert, is surprised that she is reading a book he has decided not to publish:

Emma: Why?
Robert: Oh . . . not much more to say on that subject,
        really, is there?
Emma: What do you consider the subject to be?
Robert: Betrayal.
Emma: No it isn't.
Robert: Isn't it? What is it then?
Emma: I haven't finished it yet. I'll let you know. (216)

The men in the play control words; they are publishers. In Lacan's words, they are the subject supposed to know. Emma's response, however, indicates that she has access to the same words as the men—she is not excluded from language—but she does view it differently. Moreover, Emma's reading is not definitively or rigidly closed—characteristics that many post-structuralists associate with the male, the phallocentric nature of language. Instead, her reading is open-ended. Though phallocentrism itself generally characterizes such readings as faulty or weak, Pinter's play illustrates that Emma's reading is powerful enough to make Robert reconsider: "Of course, I could be thinking of the wrong book" (216).

Pinter seems to relish making his male characters and their desire for power and mastery look foolish in this play. The entire work might even be considered Pinter's parody of patriarchy. For example, Emma is unfaithful not only to her husband but to her lover. Furthermore, she does not play any of the stereotypical roles well; she is both mother and lover, wife and whore. Her reluctance to participate in the phallic economy via such stereo-

types is made explicit. When she and Jerry separate, for instance, they talk about their love nest, the apartment they have
rented for the purpose of marital infidelity. Jerry reads Emma
stereotypically when he presumes that she wanted a "home"
with him, a repetition of her relationship with Robert. Emma,
however, makes it clear that she did not want the same kind of
home she had with Robert but something different: "It was
never intended to be the same kind of home. Was it?" (197).
Again, Emma uses words differently, seeing more to the word
home than Jerry does.

    More importantly, Emma disrupts the delicate homosocial
relationship between Robert and Jerry. Without her "in place,"
the two men can no longer relate to one another, symbolically
illustrated through Robert's discussion of the squash game.
Emma cannot attend, for the female presence would ruin everything. Tellingly, it is a letter that brings the affair to Robert's
attention. Again, Pinter symbolically connects language and
gender.

    When the two men meet after Robert's discovery, Pinter
comically exposes the loose ends that phallocentrism so desperately tries to hide. While Jerry may not know how to read
Robert at this point, the audience does, thanks to Pinter's deft
handling of dramatic irony. We know that Robert is upset by the
affair, but his attempts to hide those feelings are preposterous:
he gets drunk and takes out all his hostilities on the waiter while
treating Jerry with the utmost respect.

    Robert behaves similarly in the squash discussion. When
Emma asks if she might go along, Robert launches into a
philosophical and sociological argument against her participation, all the while seething with repressed rage. Robert treats
Emma as other, and his rage objectifies her. Jerry, however, is
left unscathed.

    However, at the end of the play, Pinter makes it clear that
Jerry initiated the affair. Jerry's look, his role as master, begins
the romance. He even tells Emma to objectify herself with his
look:

Look at the way you're looking at me. I can't wait for you,
I'm bowled over, I'm totally knocked out, you dazzle me,
you jewel, my jewel, I can't sleep again, no, listen, it's the
truth, I won't walk, I'll be a cripple, I'll descend, I'll
diminish, into total paralysis, my life is in your hands, that's
what you're banishing me to, a state of catatonia, do you know
the state of catatonia? do you? do you? the state of . . .
where the reigning prince is the prince of emptiness, the
prince of absence, the prince of desolation. I love you. (266)

Here Jerry romanticizes his own lack, but he is effectively
seducing Emma.

The issue of gender difference is explicitly expressed throughout the play, and the position of women as objects within this
phallic economy is also highlighted. "Emma seems very much
like her daughter Charlotte who was thrown up in the air as a
child and caught by Jerry in the midst of both Emma's and Jerry's
families. The image is a central one" (Burkman, "Betrayal" 511).
Both Emma and her daughter are objects to be tossed around by
men. There is no difference between them, since they are
objects. And when Jerry and Peter attempt to account for gender
difference, the fact that men are more afraid to leave the womb
than women, they conclude, tautologically, that this difference
"might have something to do with the difference between the
sexes" (205). In an ironic twist, gender difference becomes the
explanation, the existential mirror, which assures the men that
they have the correct answer, that they are in fact in control The
comic circularity of their argument, however, underscores the
fact that this autonomy is founded upon nothing.

In one of the more disturbing moments of the play, Robert
admits to hitting Emma, not because of the affair but because of
"the old itch . . . you understand" (185). Such an expression of
violence from the men in this play is uncharacteristic. The
competitive hostility they feel towards one another and towards
Emma is generally cloaked in British understatement. Surprisingly, Jerry takes this explanation as a matter of course, as
nothing out of the ordinary.

Despite Jerry's admonitions to the contrary, the play concludes with the image of Jerry and Emma facing one another eye-to-eye. Though this scene takes place in their past, with the two positioned in this way, there appears to be some ideological progress for Emma, not in terms of the history of the affair but in terms of the play's thematic concerns. Both Jerry and Emma look at each other, but because of the events that precede this moment, Pinter may be asking us to look at this image differently. In a play that is constantly reminding the male characters in particular that things are not always what they seem, Pinter appears to be presenting us with a similar reminder. In this way, the character of Emma is unfaithful in many ways. She does not read the way the men do, and she longs for a different kind of home and love. While the play concludes with a scene taken from the beginning of the affair, we know that Emma has moved on. Something is wrong with the picture.

A Kind of Alaska

If Pinter's *Homecoming* offers an illustration for female alterity in a lower-class household, *No Man's Land* an upper-class world, and *Betrayal* a middle-class existence, *A Kind of Alaska* (1981) offers an accurate metaphor for the alterity of women in general regardless of class by creating a modern version of the fairy tale "Sleeping Beauty." Based on the Brothers Grimm's "Brier Rose," the most popular version of the story has sleeping beauty awakened by a handsome prince who kisses her and whisks her off to patriarchal paradise. As the ultimate example of female spectacle, silence, and the virginal woman, the fairy tale indicates that there are great rewards for women who behave similarly within the phallic economy. Pinter's beauty, however, speaks, and through this variation, the play illustrates that neither her sleep nor her awakening permit feminine desire within patriarchy. There is no "happily ever after" for Pinter's Deborah.

As Pinter notes in an opening comment, *Alaska* was inspired by Dr. Oliver Sacks's work with patients struck by an unusual strain of sleeping sickness during World War I (3). The discovery of the drug l-dopamine fifty years later, however, awakened many of the patients, but as Sacks's research testifies, many victims, particularly Rose R. whom Sacks credits as the case that inspired Pinter, preferred sleep to drug-induced consciousness (256–57). Pinter's rare admission of source material has prompted many critics to argue that the situation of reluctant awakening provided him with the perfect opportunity to develop his usual "universal" themes such as the unreliability of memory, the problematic nature of communication, and the uncertain status of human existence and identity.[5] Admittedly, the play raises these issues, but to sacrifice the centrality of the female character in order to support "universal" considerations not only ignores the important choice Pinter made when creating the play—Sacks's study, after all, contains male patients as well as female—but it also ignores the political content of the play. The recent Hollywood movie version of Sacks's work focused on a male character, and this difference is an important one. The film, *Awakenings*, starring Robert DeNiro as a patient and Robin Williams as the doctor, focused almost exclusively on their relationship. Though endearing, the film marginalized women; they served as nurses, mothers, and patients, patients by the way, who were not as interesting as DeNiro. The film even replayed the sleeping beauty myth through a quite average nurse: for all her sacrifices for the good doctor, she is finally rewarded in the end with a date. The centrality of the female character in Pinter's play, however, leads to very different conclusions.

In fact, the centrality of the female character is crucial in Pinter's play, for *Alaska* "explores the complexities and uncertainties of being a woman or rather of becoming a woman" (Burkman, *Godot* 157). For feminists, and particularly those interested in psychoanalysis, such a process has never been apolitical, and it has rarely been the subject for Hollywood. Furthermore, *Alaska* premiered with two other plays in 1981: *Family Voices* and *Victoria Station*. Pinter entitled the event

Other Places. While the other plays do not focus on femininity, *Alaska* does, so it is difficult to ignore the title *Other Places.* Throughout the play, Pinter explores the place of the other, the place of women within a patriarchal context. Psychoanalysis is especially appropriate when approaching this play, since the situation Pinter establishes even parallels Freudian analysis: the female is diseased, "hysterical," while the doctor, the subject supposed to know, has the answers. Hélène Cixous cleverly compares the psychoanalytic situation to that of the Grimm Brothers' "Sleeping Beauty" tale. Through the character of the psychoanalytic Prince Charming, we have a

> man who will finally order woman, "set her to rights," by teaching her that without man she could "misrecognize." He will teach her the Law of the Father. Something of the order of: "Without me, without me—the Absolute—Father (the father is always that much more absolute the more he is improbable, dubious)—without me you wouldn't exist, I'll show you." ("Castration" 46)

Initially, the play leads us to believe that Hornby's desire to educate and treat Deborah is altruistically motivated. As the good doctor, he has remained with her even after her family left. The Hollywood version of Sacks's work upholds this reading: the doctor is compassionate and intensely committed to alleviating the suffering of his patients. Pinter's play, however, dispels Hornby's altruism and scientific objectivity when Hornby himself admits that he has married Deborah's sister, Pauline, then abandoned her to remain with Deborah. While these admissions may be made in order to reassure Deborah that she has been loved and taken care of during her illness, as Bernard Dukore ("Alaskan" 172) and Elizabeth Sakellaridou (210) argue, it is difficult not to question the motives of a man who has taken a comatose woman as a love object.

The situation, of course, provides Hornby with the perfect mirror; Deborah is flat, silent, and smooth as sheets. There is nothing to challenge his fantasy of autonomy. Why, then, does

Hornby awaken Deborah, this perfect mirror? As Lacan and others have noted, masculine desire shifts and the mirror image is characterized by both jubilation and despair. In effect, Hornby wants more; his desire is never satisfied. Rather than examining himself, he turns to Deborah. The "lovely injection" he administers to Deborah is highly charged sexually. It is not just a kiss that awakens Deborah but penetration. Hornby's fluid establishes a more intimate contact with his sleeping beauty. Furthermore, Hornby, who has remained with Deborah throughout her life, possesses her narrative, or so he thinks. He has nothing to fear from this awakened woman, since he possesses the story of her existence. Even his first words to her are a demand for her silence (7).

Deborah, however, will not remain silent, and she senses that there is something wrong with Hornby's explanations:

> I've obviously committed a criminal offence and am now in prison. I'm quite prepared to face up to the facts. But what offence? I can't imagine what offence it could be. I mean one that would bring . . . such a terrible sentence. (17)

As Hornby repeatedly tells her, she has been asleep. Deborah, however, cannot understand the error in that: "Why do you blame me? I was simply obeying the law of the body" (14). In a patriarchal system that has denied women access to their bodies, particularly through the medical profession, such obedience cannot be tolerated. Throughout history, the female body has symbolized nothing but chaos and evil, uncontrollable sexual desire. The medical history of hysteria, for example, blames a "wandering womb" for all female problems, which are solved by a socially, sexually, and emotionally dominant husband (Bernheimer 2–7). By obeying the law of body, Deborah has committed a crime, and now she must be educated in the law of Hornby, the law of the father, the law of patriarchy.

Interestingly, Deborah's explanations for her condition cast her in a passive role. They sound strangely like Harlequin romance novels. She thinks that she has been kidnapped, even raped. On the one hand, these somewhat adolescent fantasies may illustrate the point at which Deborah's female development stopped, and from Hornby's viewpoint, these narratives are insufficient, not right. Deborah's stories appear diseased, while Hornby's appear truthful, logical, and scientific. On the other hand, Deborah's narratives, albeit limited, silence Hornby, nd she revels in her own voice, thereby challenging the acquiescent role of women. Further, through the tale-telling process, not Hornby's direction, Deborah concludes that the narratives are inadequate, but perhaps for a different reason than Hornby. During one fantasy, for example, she indicates that the passive position of women in these stories separates her from her own desire: "My lust was my own. I kept it by me. You took it from me" (12). She concludes saying that she sounds "childish" and "out of tune" (12). Through this juxtaposition, the play undercuts the usefulness of such explanations of Deborah's situation because they require that Deborah deny her desire and remain passive in the presence of a swashbuckling male. In this way, the play offers two interpretations of a text, and although both readers come to similar conclusions, the motives underlying their reading process constitute the gender conflict that underpins the play. Hornby dismisses the value of the narratives because they complicate his desire to control Deborah's identity, while Deborah's attitude toward these narratives shifts. She realizes that the stories that shape her understanding of herself are insufficient because they, too, deny her identity. As Tania Modleski notes in her study of Harlequin romances,

> Even though the novels can be said to intensify female tensions and conflicts, on balance the contradictions in women's lives are more responsible for the existence of Harlequins than Harlequins are for the contradictions. (57)

Hornby's treatment of Pauline, moreover, solidifies his role as a menacing presence in the play. Pauline does not fulfill his expectations, and Hornby is clearly irritated when she enters the room without gaining his permission (26). Later Pauline asks him what she should say. He asserts she should tell both lies and truth (27). Hornby is clearly in charge. He is the arbiter of value, power, and language in this situation.

Deborah, too, focuses on Pauline as a female object. She is shocked that Pauline has breasts and suddenly discovers her own. Both Pauline and Hornby tell her she is woman, and she retreats to her bed in terror. The implications of this response are difficult to miss: a forty-five-year-old virgin, a woman who has slept through her reproductive years, suddenly discovers her own femininity. Her reaction is not one of joy but of terror. Given the manner in which Hornby treats Pauline, such a retreat is justified. There are no rewards for women in this patriarchal economy.

By positioning Deborah's description of her somnambulant state at the end of the play, Pinter not only demonstrates that Deborah has in fact suffered, but he also forces a comparison between Deborah's awakened and sleeping states. Deborah tells us that she has been imprisoned in an endless hall of mirrors, a prisoner of reflection. Given her "education" through-out the play, however, an education that asks her to abandon her narratives and her identity in order to accept her womanliness, Pinter may be asking us to note that the alternative Hornby offers Deborah is just a new "kind of Alaska." Mirrors entombed her during her sleep, and female stereotypes threaten to en-tomb her now.

The play concludes with Deborah coming to terms with her new role and preparing for a "birthday party" that celebrates her birth into patriarchy. One of the important issues the play raises concerns the quality of life Deborah will have now that she has lost her memory and much of her life. In other awaken-ing stories, life is usually better after the period of sleep. In his work on the fairy tale "Sleeping Beauty," for example, Bruno Bettelheim argues that

> while many fairy tales stress great deeds the heroes must perform to become themselves, "The Sleeping Beauty"

emphasizes the long, quiet concentration on oneself that is
also needed. During the months before the first menstruation, and often also for some time immediately following it,
girls are passive, seem sleepy, and withdraw into themselves. While no equally noticeable state heralds the coming of sexual maturity in boys, many of them experience a
period of lassitude and of turning inward during puberty
which equals the female experience. . . . In major life
changes such as adolescence, for successful growth oppor-
tunities both active and quiescent periods are needed.
(225)

Deborah's quiet period, however, has not been restful. As she
tells Pauline and Hornby, it was a kind of torture. As female
spectacle, the object of the male look, Deborah has suffered.
Her awakening, moreover, does not appear much better—there
is no handsome prince or even a happy family to welcome her
into the world. Instead she is told lies and truths, promised a
pathetic birthday party, and given numerous rules for behavior.

In Oliver Sacks's *Awakenings*, which inspired Pinter's play,
the young woman who is the prototype for Deborah fares no
better. Like Deborah, Rose R. was a promising, young, intel-
ligent woman when the illness struck her. For forty-three years
she was in a trancelike state, though she had the ability to speak,
unlike Deborah. When she could speak, her conversations echo
Deborah and Hornby's dialogues. When asked what it was like
to think of nothing, which she thought of a great deal of the time,
she says:

> Worlds within worlds within worlds within worlds. Once I
> get going I can't possibly stop. It's like being caught be-
> tween mirrors, or echoes, or something. Or being caught
> on a merry-go-round which won't come to a stop. (69)

Her immediate response to the wonder cure, l-dopamine, was
similar to Deborah's—euphoric, adolescent, hopeful. But as the
treatment progressed, she lost control. The drug therapy did
not work for her, and she began losing motor control, as well as

her mental capacities. Sacks concludes his study in awe of the disease that keeps such a normal and lively personality trapped. He even likens her to the fairy tale princess: "She is a Sleeping Beauty whose 'awakening' was unbearable to her, and who will never be awakened again" (79).

Surprisingly, Pinter is not the only dramatist to demonstrate the ill-effects of this disease. Sam Shepard's *La Turista* (1968) (which moves in reverse chronological order, as does Pinter's *Betrayal*), also contains a victim of this strange sleeping sickness. In Shepard's play, however, the victim is a man, and when the doctors threaten to impose social restrictions upon him, he leaves the scene by jumping through a wall. And although the young man, Gaston, in Jean Anouilh's *Traveller Without Luggage* (1937) may not have the identical disease that Shepard's Kent and Pinter's Deborah have, he has suffered amnesia, and the entire play revolves around his quest for his identity and the other characters' desire to force him to choose the identity they have constructed for him. In the end, Gaston discovers his family but chooses another, more suitable one for himself. Unlike Deborah, these male somnambulists have a choice regarding their identities.

Pinter's play concludes by finalizing Deborah's existential education. As she tells Hornby and Pauline:

> You say I have been asleep. You say I am now awake. You say I have not awoken from the dead. You say I was not dreaming then and am not dreaming now. You say I have always been alive and am alive now. You say I am a woman. . . . I think I have the matter in proportion. (*Pause*) Thank you. (40)

Of course, the speech reflects the tenuous nature of the human condition—what is consciousness and what is not—but by including the question of femininity, Pinter also raises the question of gender's role in this "universal" condition. Having listened to Pauline and Hornby throughout the course of the play, Deborah now remains disturbingly silent. In many ways, Deborah ends as she began, laying quietly on the bed, a spectacle for Hornby's look and ours. Such positioning leaves Deborah a mystery, an enigma, a sphinx. According to Hélène Cixous, "not knowing is threatening" to patriarchy, while at the same time this enigma of woman reinforces the

> desire to know. So in the end woman, in man's desire, stands in the place of not knowing, the place of mystery. In this sense she is no good, but at the same time she is good because it's this mystery that leads man to keep overcoming, dominating, subduing, putting his manhood to the test, against the mystery he has to keep forcing back. ("Castration" 49)

In this way, Deborah's ambiguous future at the end of the play at once challenges and upholds the patriarchal desire for closure.

Hornby has succeeded in recreating his "sleeping beauty." Deborah's jubilation, her narration, and her voice are now absent. This new order of consciousness offers no change; she ends as she began—silent and bedridden, a grim depiction of the effects such cultural expectations have had upon Deborah. As she told Hornby, however, she has a "laughing nature," and she has learned to dance in "narrow spaces," perhaps Pinter's hint at hope for the oppressed position of women he has so exquisitely depicted throughout the play. The place of the other, this "kind of Alaska," has some cracks.

4

"Fire in the Snow"
Shepard's Female Saviors

> Ya' see that picture over there? Ya' see that? Ya' know who
> that is? That's the woman of my dreams. That's who that is.
> She's all mine. Forever.
> —Old Man in Shepard's *Fool for Love*

SAM SHEPARD'S work coincides with one of the most exciting
periods of the feminist movement since Seneca Falls. Though far
from uncomplicated or triumphantly successful, the women's
movement throughout the sixties and seventies brought significant changes in the roles, perceptions, and representation of
women. The Roe versus Wade decision of 1973 and the perfection and widespread availability of many birth control devices
made it possible for women to control their reproductive rights,
giving them greater latitude in decisions regarding motherhood. For many women, this freedom gave them the time to
pursue political, economic, and social advances. During the
seventies, "women advocated day care, part-time work, pregnancy and parenting leaves, flextime, and job sharing to close
the gap between home and work" (Klein 170). Women also
finally gained success in the areas of "sports, politics, television,
and film" (Wandersee 150). While the media often manipulated
the images of the liberated woman to create a superwoman, it
did offer women role models for working, single women.

While O'Neill's biography and work suggest his sympathy
toward women's rights and while Pinter repeatedly defends his
female characters against male-biased critics who oppose female characterization that violates traditional expectations, for

many feminists, Sam Shepard symbolizes the dramatic backlash to these feminist cultural and political gains. Many of his early works seem to revel in male violence. The media has represented Shepard as a "Marlboro man," and Shepard himself appears to perpetuate this "lone cowboy role" (Hart, "Fool" 217). The media has characterized him as theatre's version of Clint Eastwood's high plains drifter, a man who does not take the beaten path of Broadway, but instead blazes a trail elsewhere.[1] In his early interviews, Shepard even disavowed the need to revise his work; it came to him as quickly and fully formed as the mythical Eastwood character came from the desert landscape. To Shepard's credit, in his later "*True West* Interviews," he admitted that during that time, he was basically lazy (60).

Although there is some debate concerning female representation in his early plays, Shepard tends to present the action from a male perspective while ignoring female characterization. Felicia Hardison Londré calls these early plays Shepard's "mindless macho period" (20). In her 1981 collection, Bonnie Marranca even threatens him with anonymity if he does not revise his presentations of femininity ("Shepard" 84–85). Florence Falk concurs:

> In the plays of Sam Shepard, the cowboy is the reigning male; consequently, *any* female is, perforce, marginalized. . . . No other figure [Shepard] so successfully sustains, recycles—and condones—the violence this cowboy is bred on.[2] (91)

In these early plays women are props for male performances; mothers merely highlight the complicated oedipal relationships between fathers and sons; and men frequently must escape the clutches of a spoiled, sexually and emotionally demanding female.

Strongly influenced by the rock culture of the sixties, Shepard's plays at this time were also highly experimental. Characters shifted from persona to persona at breakneck speed.

While Pinter . . . allows his characters to seem to control
his play's filmic, fluid action, Shepard wrenches his characters from one transformation to another, clearly denying
them the choice of options that Pinter's characters ponder
during their pauses and silences. (Cima 73)

While this statement does not imply that Pinter's characters are
more in control of their identities, it does indicate a significant
difference between the two playwrights: Pinter's characters
ponder, while Shepard's violently emote. Moreover, the women
in Shepard's early plays generally either prompt the violent
quest or remain in the background while wild cowboys take
center stage, destroying everything in sight.

Whether Shepard's time in England domesticated his dramas is difficult to say, but upon his return to the United States,
his work takes a noticeably different turn. Family becomes his
focus, and many of his female characters are developed in ways
never seen before in a Shepard piece. Although he began
working with Joe Chaikin's Open Theatre, which focused on the
fluidity of character and action and which prompted him to
place these unusual characters in unusual settings, Shepard's
more recent work has taken these experiments and placed them
in more staid, domestic settings. Lynda Hart argues that this
strategy, combining the familiar setting with unfamiliar modes
of characterization, "are constitutive of some feminist theatre,"
but the Open Theatre and Shepard failed to utilize these
strategies to disrupt sexual difference ("*Fool*" 216). She continues, arguing that Shepard's "recuperation of realism coincides
precisely with his rise to critical acclaim and the concomitant,
coterminus, full blown expression of his misogyny and gyno-
phobia" ("*Fool*" 217).

Admittedly, Shepard's most publicized early attempt at
domestic drama did not result in a reconsideration of female
characterization. *The Curse of the Starving Class* (1977) is
riddled with contradictory and often simplistic representations
of female characters. The family is cursed by an uncontrollable
fate that results in the characters' inability to love. This curse is

likened to the "curse" of menstruation, and the play represents
such blood as somehow defiled. Despite the play's attempts to
blame the father's blood for this curse involving an inability to
love, it is implied that the female also brings a disease into the
home. The play concludes in oedipal triumph. The son, who has
been purified throughout the action of the play, now takes the
father's place with his mother, perhaps on the edge of a new,
incestuous Eden.

However, some evidence suggests that Shepard began consciously reconsidering his representation of female characters
after this play. According to director Robert Woodruff, the first
draft of *Buried Child* (1979) did not present females in any better
or significant light, particularly the character of Shelly. Through
the production process, however, Woodruff and the cast encouraged Shepard to give Shelly greater depth (156). As the draft at
Boston University's library and Charles Whiting's analysis of
those scripts attest, Shelly was merely another version of the
spoiled whore from Shepard's early and offensive work, *Shaved
Splits* (1969) in the early draft (Whiting, "Digging Up"). However, as a result of the comments of actress Betsy Scott, Shepard
revised the character to make her less stereotypical.

Furthermore, during an interview with Michiko Kakutani
in 1984, Shepard offered an insightful and far from flattering
description of masculine violence:

> I think there's something about American violence that to
> me is very touching. . . . In full force it's very ugly, but
> there's also something very moving about it, because it has
> to do with humiliation. There's some hidden, deeply rooted
> thing in the Anglo-male American that has to do with
> inferiority, that has to do with not being a man, and always,
> continually having to act out some idea of manhood that is
> invariably violent. This sense of failure runs very deep.
> ("Myths" 26)

While this sense of inferiority does not excuse the behavior,
Shepard's perception of violence is complex and articulates very

clearly the Lacanian concept of lack. Male violence and aggression becomes one of the worst extremes of the desire for power, autonomy, and female obedience. More importantly, Shepard's insight here indicates that male violence stems from the male, not from the female victim. And while some of Shepard's men may blame their female counterparts for their violent outbursts, here Shepard indicates that he does not.

Perhaps the difficulty with Shepard's plays and his female characters results from the tension surrounding the issues his plays present. As Herbert Blau notes during his discussion of *Buried Child*, Shepard wants simultaneously to dismantle the family and to keep "the institution intact" (527). C. W. E. Bigsby argues that the contradictions in Shepard "are presumably what keeps Shepard writing. The persistence of hope is indeed a fundamental condition and definitional quality of the absurd" (243). Contrary to the views of many feminist critics writing on Shepard today, in his later plays, Shepard in fact depicts the quest for masculine power as deplorable or ridiculous, while he presents the female characters sympathetically. The female characters are frequently represented as the calm amidst the macho storms, frequently offering flexibility in the face of destructive male rigidity. Such gender representation, of course, borders on the Madonna image, particularly the view that women are somehow the repositories of morality.

Shepard's contact with actresses like Betsy Scott as well as his relationship with Jessica Lange, which ended his marriage to O-Lan, may have altered Shepard's view of women, and much has been made of Lange's effects on his work as an actor.[3] But like the biographies of O'Neill and Pinter, Shepard's biography also, remarkably, contains a story about his response to his image in a mirror, an anecdote illustrating that Shepard's recent representations of women stem from a time before his relationships with O-Lan, Lange, and other female performers. According to Don Shewey's biography of Shepard, Shepard spent a great deal of time looking at himself in the mirror in 1977 observing "how his right eye was more open than his left and speculating that the good eye came from his mother, the bad eye from his father" (125). Unlike O'Neill, who used the mirror to confirm his identity, Shepard, to some extent like Pinter, notices not his autonomy but his fragmentation. More importantly, the assumption that the "good" is associated with the feminine, the "bad" with the masculine reflects many of his later representations of gender.

The fluid method of characterization, which Shepard experimented with in his earlier plays, appears to have influenced his representations of women. All the characters shift roles and personae at breakneck speed, but only the male characters presume that if they just work hard enough, an autonomous identity will appear. Male demonstrations of this assumption are frequently related to power; their chameleon-like personalities are frequently used to oppress. More importantly, this fluid method of characterization does not solidify female representation into feminine stereotypes.

The persistent image of the frontier in all Shepard's plays is also problematic in terms of gender. For many Shepard men, particularly in the earlier plays, when women and violence do nothing to alleviate their lack, they head to the great frontier. Given the work of Annette Kolodny on the narratives of female frontierswomen, this choice has repercussions regarding gender. According to Kolodny, the American frontier was "feminized." The rhetoric of the frontier described the land in terms of the female body. With the myth of the American Adam, "Eve could only be redundant" (*Land* 5). Many of Shepard's early male characters share in this belief. By removing themselves from domestic settings, responsibilities, and women, they are free to roam the prairies and discover their true identities, unfettered by social and cultural norms.[4]

In Shepard's later plays, however, many male characters return from the frontier to the domestic realm, and although Shepard does not entirely abandon the ideal of the frontier, it has gone through modifications. In *A Lie of the Mind* (1985), for example, women, not men, leave their homes in order to search for a new life "out there." Perhaps the most important variation on this theme occurs in the film *Paris, Texas* (1984) directed by Wim Wenders. The male character, appropriately named Travis, travels throughout the film, and this pilgrimage leads him to his wife, Jane. The term *pilgrimage* is appropriate, since, as we learn later in the film, Travis has made this journey as a kind of penance for his previous violent treatment of Jane. At first he guarded her jealously, then he tied a cow bell to her leg to keep her from running away, and finally he tied her to the kitchen stove with his belt. Travis makes his amends to Jane, but he realizes he cannot remain with her because he believes he will never let her be free. He will always try to possess her. In this way, the frontier becomes Travis's purgatory, a desolate world without women. As he tells Jane, he longs for "a vast country . . . somewhere without language or streets" (92). The final image the film leaves us with, however, is not an idyllic world without women, but a man lost in the desert due to his inability to accept female desires.

Buried Child

With *Buried Child* (1979), Shepard creates a contemporary American "homecoming," another "long day's journey into night." As in O'Neill's play, in Shepard's play a family secret is explored and finally exposed. And as in both O'Neill's and Pinter's plays, a woman disrupts the familial equilibrium. While Shepard is very concerned with the question of male violence, in *Buried Child*, he also explores the nature of paternity. In the end, *Buried Child* demonstrates that the law of the father is oppressive and that the family it creates is dysfunctional and violent. The men in the play are clearly linked to the darker aspects of human behavior. Dodge, the patriarch, attempts to control the workings of the house from the living room sofa, but he is old, feeble, and impotent. If we miss the imagery, his wife, Halie, who is dressed in mourning at the beginning of the play, frequently refers to him as a corpse. The two sons, Tilden and Bradley, are not characterized very differently: one is a half-wit and the other is a menace with a wooden leg. The disparity between the people and the lush vegetables Tilden brings home is clear. Shepard's imagery is unmistakable; this middle-class home is the house of the dead.

And yet, throughout the play, the characters cling to this male wasteland, its forms and its laws. Even the female character, Halie, is entangled in patriarchal expectations. She is clearly dissatisfied with her relationship to Dodge at the beginning of the play, but rather than attempting to change her relationship to men in general, she transfers her affections to other men, first to her son Ansel and then to a "father of the church" after Ansel's death. While she may not fully participate in the specific workings of her domestic patriarchy, she is still male-identified, leaving the home to erect monuments in their honor and to search for more suitable male companionship. Despite all the evidence the play presents regarding the patriarchy's impotence, Halie continues to search for a man who will satisfy her.

Her son Vince returns home, hoping to find a sense of himself, but with the mother absent, no one recognizes him. The men have nothing to offer Vince. His female companion, Shelly, also expects that the family will live up to her Norman Rockwell type expectations: home is the site of sustenance and love. But as soon as Shelly enters the home, she realizes that none of her expectations will be fulfilled. Because Shelly is an outsider, though, she is a "nice door for the audience" (Woodruff 155). Through her character, we see the dysfunctional nature of this home. It would appear, then, that Shelly gains status as a spectator, the possessor of the look. As an outsider, she watches, observes, and objectifies the action of the play. However, she is not entirely privileged, for she is part of the play. She does not entirely occupy the masculine position of spectator, for as character, she is herself spectacle. What is important, however, is that Shepard has the audience identify with a female character here, perhaps another strategy that undercuts the power of the

men in the play. Shelly sees more clearly than the other characters who are caught up in the operations of a dead system and
institution. Ironically, Shelly uses conventional female domestic activities to defend herself from her odd surroundings.
When Vince turns to her for the existential reassurance his
family cannot provide, Shelly deflects his objectifying desire by
telling him: "You're the one who wants to stay. So I'll stay. I'll
stay and I'll cut carrots. And I'll cook the carrots. And I'll do
whatever I have to do to survive. Just to make it through this"
(94). These "feminine" activities provide sustenance to Shelly.
However, for Vince they appear trivial. For reassurance, he
turns to the family photo album, framed familial objects from
the past. Even though he holds the script, it is not enough, so he
takes off for the great outdoors in search of his identity that no
one in the home will confirm.

With Vince absent, the eccentric behavior of the men
intensifies. All of them want Shelly's attention; all of them want
Shelly to mirror their desires. Tilden, for example, wants Shelly
to remain silent and listen to his story about the dead baby.
Dodge wants her to wait on him. And when Bradley tells her to
"stay put," he symbolically rapes her by putting his hand in her
mouth. The gesture is a disturbing one, but because Bradley
uses a prosthetic penis, his hand, his patriarchal power is
questioned at the very moment he is trying to prove his potency.
Later, his impotence is confirmed. Shelly manipulates and
torments him by taking away his artificial leg.

When Halie returns in the third act, she not only finds
Shelly in control, but she herself has undergone a miraculous
transformation. She is lively and out of mourning. Her change,
however, is only superficial. She is still male-identified, and her
male companion, Father Dewis, is impotent, too. As he tells
her, he cannot accommodate experiences that fall beyond his
"parish" (126).

Halie's loyalty to men and to this family is particularly
disturbing, given the confession Dodge makes in the third act.
We learn that Halie had a baby late in life, when Dodge and she

had not been sleeping together. There is even some hint that the baby was born out of a relationship between Halie and Tilden. The hint of the violation of the incest taboo is an important one, since it, according to Lévi-Strauss and Friedrich Engels is the founding principle of patriarchy (Lévi-Strauss 36; Engels 94–146). The fact that women were always sure of their offspring but men were not resulted in rigorous legislation and oppression of female sexuality and the construction of the incest taboo. Whether the incestuous relationship actually occurred is never entirely revealed, but the violation, incestuous or not, is great and symbolic of the threat feminine sexuality poses for patriarchy.

As a mother within the phallic economy, Halie had an obligation to fulfill—to insure the patriarchal lineage and retain its purity. Halie, a mother, must have a man, either a husband or son, in order to exist within the phallic economy. While upholding the prescribed desires for women in patriarchy, Halie has also violated them by taking the patriarchal admonitions too far. She must bear a son, not copulate with one. Therefore, she must be punished. Dodge mentions that he forced Halie to give birth at home in order to make delivery painful. Because the child's conception was so "unnatural," Dodge did not expect the child to live. When it does, Dodge "drowned it. Just like the runt of the litter" (124). Halie may be the keeper of the family tree, but she cannot add new branches without the law of the father.

The decision to kill Halie's child illustrates that anything created outside the father's control is nonexistent. Further, since it was a male child, Dodge has again castrated Halie, depriving her of the usual reward for women in patriarchy. By taking the child away, Dodge forces Halie outside of the phallic economy. This act may explain Halie's obsession with replacement masculine figures. She attaches herself desperately to the cultural trappings of patriarchy—monuments, priests, and her remaining sons—in order to fulfill this double castration, this double lack that Dodge has forced upon her.

Soon after this confession, Vince arrives, another half-drowned, half-drunk son who has now decided to remain in the home after Dodge's death. Shelly is shocked by his decision, but during his time in the wilderness, he realized that he was mystically and fatally connected to his family. As he tells Shelly:

I could see myself in the windshield. My face. My eyes. I studied my face. Studied everything about it. As though I was looking at another man. As though I could see his whole race behind him. Like a mummy's face. I saw him dead and alive at the same time. In the same breath. In the windshield I watched him breathe as though he was frozen in time. And every breath marked him. Marked him forever without him knowing. And then his face changed. His face became his father's face. Same bones. Same eyes. Same nose. Same breath. And his father's face changed to his Grandfather's face. And it went on like that. Changing. Clear on back to faces I'd never seen before but still recognized. Still I recognized the bones underneath. The eyes. The breath. . . . Then it all dissolved. Everything dissolved. (130)

Ironically, Vince's attempts to run away from his family in order to discover his identity bring him to the realization that he is connected to that family, that his identity is intricately bound to the bones of this family, notably the male bones. While looking in the mirror, Vince has discovered an even better device with which to gain a sense of self, complete, whole, and historical—through the patriarchal line. The dissolution at the end, however, presents a threat, and it brings Vince back to his home and informs his decision to remain—he will stop the dissolution by taking Dodge's place, by making the choice that will perpetuate the patriarchy. He has discovered his masculine mission.

However, this solution is undercut when Vince takes Dodge's place on the family sofa. It has not been a place of life throughout the play; it has, instead, signified death. Shelly, whom Dodge referred to as a "hoper," a life-affirming person, can no longer remain with Vince in his house of the dead, and she leaves, not in the hopes of finding an identity on the frontier, but in order to escape the deathly cloying familial relationships. Shelly leaves the house to enter the world of light.

The final image of the play underscores the home's sepulchral atmosphere. Its inhabitants can only see the sun from their windows, while Tilden resurrects the tiny decaying corpse of the "buried child" and returns it to Halie, the "keeper of the corpses." The images of regeneration that surround the house only serve to heighten the decay within: the family's heinous crimes, the violence of the patriarchal system, and the contradictory expectations placed upon women within a patriarchal economy.

True West

Sam Shepard's *True West* (1980), a raucous male wasteland is Shepard's comedy of male manners. Unlike O'Neill's *Iceman* and Pinter's *No Man's Land*, *True West* clearly illustrates that the violent and often comic duel between Lee and Austin takes place on maternal turf. "Mom's" absence throughout most of the play is the foundation upon which the brotherly feud is staged. The quest for identity, the search for the "true west," a "real man," and a resolution to the dialectically opposed issues raised throughout the play require the obliteration of the mother's place. Generically named "Mom," this absent female character has taken a vacation to Alaska. This location, as well as her stereotypical representation by her sons, indicates that she occupies both a literal and figurative "kind of Alaska" in the play. Further, while the play admittedly celebrates the destruction, it also underscores the futility of violent masculine behavior.

Austin, a Hollywood scriptwriter, has returned to his mother's house to find inspiration for his new screenplay. Lee, who has lived on the desert for years, has returned to find financial assistance, determined to steal from the neighborhood and his mother's home. For both men, the absent female is so profitable that an oedipal duel ensues based on the fraternal rights to the home. Each brother believes that he is the sole inheritor of the maternal, and each believes that the winner of the battle is the "real man."

The play begins by establishing the brothers' differences. Austin represents the social order, while Lee represents the wilds of nature. When, for example, Austin says he cannot turn Lee in to the police because Lee is his brother, his belief in familial forms overrides his sense of social law. Lee, on the other hand, challenges Austin's assumptions about family by reminding him of the "natural" forces that inform even this institution:

> Family people. Brothers. Brothers-in-law. Cousins. Real American-type people. They kill each other in the heat mostly. In the Smog-Alerts. In the Brush Fire Season. Right about this time a' year. (24)

However, the play gradually strips away the brothers' differences, and by the end, Saul Kimmer, the Hollywood producer, cannot even tell the men apart. Both men have confessed their dissatisfaction with their current situations: Austin is dying in the city, while Lee aimlessly wanders the desert only because he cannot live in society, not because of some mythic fulfillment. Both look for something; both are lacking; but both dream of some "thing," some *petit objet a* that will fulfill them, and by the end of the play, it becomes the life-style of the other brother.

As in Pinter's *No Man's Land*, in *True West* questions regarding gender and male autonomy in particular are intimately connected to the symbolic, the world of words and culture. Initially, Austin controls the Hollywood script, and he defends his rights by arguing that he is an artist, somehow above the common fray. But Lee attacks Austin's pristine position when Austin mentions that he has some business to attend to regarding the script and a Hollywood producer: "I thought it was 'Art' you were doin'" (14). Lee implies that Austin is not the sole creator of the script, not a "real man," but instead a linguistic errand boy engaged in business not art. He, on the other hand, has a script that is "real commercial" and "true-to-life" (15). Lee uses the same approach when the brothers discuss the nature of the true west: Austin does not know, while Lee presents himself as the phallus, the subject supposed to know.

He understands the delicate distinctions between the symbolic
(reality) and the imaginary (fiction) while Austin does not.

Placing such arguments in the mouths of men like Lee, a
bum, and Austin, a Hollywood hackwriter, is the source of much
of the play's humor. Issues that engage the great minds of
literary criticism now befuddle Lee and Austin. More importantly, Shepard complicates the discussion by placing the question of fictional characters in the mouths of fictional characters.
This philosophical and representational Chinesebox makes the
search for truth regarding fiction almost impossible to locate.
When Lee and Austin begin working on the script, for example,
Lee's ideas grow more and more preposterous—two men relentlessly chase one another across the desert. To Austin, who is
well versed in narrative form, the idea fluctuates between the
clichéd and the absurd. Lee's explanation, however, reflects the
relationship of the two brothers on stage, thereby making his
fictional script real. As he tells Austin, the two characters in his
script:

> take off after each other straight into an endless black
> prairie. The sun is just comin' down and they can feel the
> night on their backs. What they don't know is that each one
> of 'em is afraid, see. Each one separately thinks that he's the
> only one that's afraid. And they keep ridin' like that straight
> into the night. Not knowing. And the one who's chasin'
> doesn't know where the other one is taking him. And the
> one who's being chased doesn't know where he's going. (27)

This quest, too, is motivated by an absent woman, for the
one man chases the other because he has been sleeping with his
wife. Shepard's image very poetically summarizes Lacan's theories regarding the essential lack that characterizes human existence. Without the presence of a woman, the men are lost,
ostensibly defending their rights, but finally the chase creates
the illusion of some sort of meaning to their meaningless exis-
tences. In this image, the chase becomes the mirror by which
the men attempt to gain a sense of identity. Saul Kimmer's

enthusiasm for Lee's script indicates that this quest is not limited to the two brothers. Instead, the script is marketable, fodder for popular culture.

To complicate the established opposition between art and reality, the play itself contains a true story from Shepard's past (Shewey 140–41). The story about the brothers' father losing his teeth apparently happened to Shepard and his own father. Again, the man is characterized as lost and searching, in this case for a new set of false teeth. Once he gains this *petit objet a*, however, he does not use the teeth and leaves them in a bar. Lee uses this story to justify his plans to give his father the financial proceeds from his screenplay. Again, the mother's needs and the mother's place do not enter into his own version of the phallic economy.

When Mom does arrive, she appears just as Lee and Austin have "scripted" her—a mother, not an individual, and both men react to her in this way: they behave like little children caught in mischievous acts. The mother's position as defender of social values is confirmed.

> Mom is a bizarre creature to say the least: wearing a white suit, a silver wig and huge mother-of-pearl earrings, she has scarlet lips and a matching red suitcase. In a daze, she walks through her littered kitchen and inspects the now dead plants hanging in the windows. The effect is chilling and the two brothers react, at first, like kids about to be spanked. (Kleb 119)

Mom's dazed condition suggests that she "is infected with what Shepard considers the most serious new-western sickness— alienation from the land. No wonder she seems flat, remote, lifeless, and unreal" (Kleb 122–23). Admittedly, Mom is a problematic character, but Shepard has complicated our expectations concerning the wild or true west, so it is difficult to see how Mom reflects the misuse or ignorance of the land. Moreover, she has vacationed in Alaska, one of the few places still considered a "frontier" in American culture.

For others, this character merely reflects Shepard's inability to draw fully developed female characters, but the scene disturbs the expectations the play has set up regarding the character of Mom. As a stereotypical mother, she should function as an emotional and spiritual housekeeper, a Mom ex machina, who will clean up the boy's lives, as well as her home. But this Mom does nothing. According to Luce Irigaray, doing nothing is a feminist strategy for change. She tells women to stop trying:

> You have been taught that you were property, private or public, belonging to one man or all. To family, tribe, State, even a Republic. That therein lay your pleasure. And that, unless you gave in to man's, or men's, desires, you would not know sexual pleasure. . . . Don't force yourselves to repeat, don't congeal your dreams or desires in unique and definitive representations. You have so many continents to explore that if you set up borders for yourselves you won't be able to "enjoy" all of your own "nature." (*This Sex* 203–4)

As Shepard's play indicates, Mom is clearly upset by the fact that her boys have destructively erased her space, but this Mom with a difference will not provide existential reassurance, let alone do housework.

Mom, however, is not an entirely radical figure at the close of the play. She encourages Austin to remain because he has a family, thereby upholding the social order. Her own view of the art versus reality question, while offering an alternative to Lee's and Austin's solution, is based on her own inability to distinguish between the two. She misreads an announcement advertising a Picasso exhibit as an announcement for his actual appearance. When Austin tells her, "Picasso's dead, Mom" (54), she is devastated. During her Alaskan vacation, she despaired: "It was the worst feeling being up there. In Alaska. Staring out a window. I never felt so desperate before. That's why when I saw that article on Picasso I thought—" (59). Mom never does finish her sentence, but she clearly seeks solace from her desperation through a man, an artistic "authority." She senses her discomfort, but she does not have the means available for an alternative, so she resorts to the expected feminine response in the phallic economy, a man. However, when Austin orders her to stay because "this is where you live," she responds, "I don't recognize it at all" (59). In these final moments, Austin and Lee try to persuade her to see the situation through their eyes, but with this concluding sentence, the play implies that Mom sees the situation for herself. Her look determines her next course of action, not the look of the men. She leaves the house, letting the brothers battle on their own.

It appears at the end, however, that Austin has won. Lee seems to be dead, but just as the play is about to close, Lee jumps up, and the battle begins again. The play closes with the brothers facing each other, mirror images, each man desperately wanting the other to mirror his desires. In this way, Shepard dramatizes the ideological and emotional motives underlying male violence. Since the game persists endlessly, moreover, the play also underscores its futility.

A Lie of the Mind

When Shepard's *Lie of the Mind* appeared on off Broadway in 1986, most audiences and reviewers agreed—the women in the play made significant contributions to the drama as a whole and were central to its action and success. They had the funniest lines and an independence of spirit that many believed had been lacking throughout Shepard's work. Ironically, many also chastised Shepard for "selling out"; they yearned for his "mindless macho period."[4] A few critics, however, were not convinced that Shepard had really renounced his misogynistic ways entirely. Lynda Hart, for example, argues that while this play "contained squarely within the arena of gender conflict; but the origin of the conflict is in the father's relationship with his son" (*Metaphorical Stages* 107). Hart implies that Shepard is merely cashing in on "political correctness." Admittedly, Shepard's work from its beginning through plays such as *Rock Garden* (1964) to his current work explores the father-son relationship with almost obsessive repetition. In his later works, however, the mother's role and importance are made more explicit. In *A Lie of the Mind*, in particular, the main character, Jake, may struggle with his father figure, but through the course of the play, Shepard not only exposes this obsession as futile but also pays close attention to a mother-daughter relationship. And although the mother and the daughter may not be the primary characters in the play, it is their relationship that changes throughout the drama and that offers one of the few healing images in a play racked by physical and emotional disease. Moreover, Shepard once again explores and exposes the masculine myth of autonomy and the violence with which many of the characters pursue this myth. In the end, this quest becomes merely "a lie of the mind."

Shepard opens the play with an epigram which reflects some of the thematic issues of the play:

> Something identifies you with the one who leaves you, and it is your common power to return: thus your greatest sorrow.

> Something separates you from the one who remains with you, and it is your common slavery to depart: thus your meagerest rejoicing.

With this quotation from Cesar Vallejo, Shepard concisely articulates that aspect of the human condition he will illustrate throughout the play, one surprisingly similar to Lacan's formulations regarding the split subject: separate human beings yearn for unity and completion, looking to an other for fulfillment. The entire structure of the play highlights this idea. The play is divided into alternating scenes between Jake's family and Beth's family. Such a structure, of course, reflects Beth and Jake's physical separation, but it also highlights the generic separation of the sexes. The imaginary illusion of unification, however, persists in the minds of many of the characters. Although the two lovers' families never come together, Beth and Jake in the early scenes possess some mystical, nonverbal means of communication and connection. Shepard highlights this illusion through his directorial comments regarding light and sound techniques, which connect the disparate elements of the play. The characters' behavior throughout the play, however, undercuts this imaginary sense of unity.

The play opens with Jake and his brother Frankie trying to make a connection via the telephone. Admittedly, the technique is a bit clumsy and reminiscent of television dramas — and it is difficult to say whether Shepard opens with this time-worn strategy because he wishes to establish conventional expectations in his audience or because it works. In any case, this sort of choice has led critics to claim that Shepard is now pandering to the "lowest common denominator." In the end, the exposition works, no matter how clumsy, and we learn that Jake has beaten Beth so badly that he thinks she is dead.

As we learn in the third scene, Jake beat Beth because she was not cooperating; she was not fulfilling her role as a dutiful wife. As he tells his brother Frankie, she was beginning to work as an actress, dressing the part of a prostitute, not a dutiful female lover. Consequently, Jake concludes that Beth is a whore, a destructive female, unfaithful to the ways of the phallic economy:

> Woman starts dressin' more and more skimpy every time she goes out. Starts puttin' on more and more smells. Oils. She was always oiling herself before she went out. Every morning. Smell would wake me up. Coconut or Butterscotch or some goddamn thing. Sweet stuff. . . . I'd watch her oiling herself while I pretended to be asleep. She was in a dream, the way she did it. Like she was imagining someone else touching her. (8)

In the second scene, Shepard established Beth's obsessive loyalty to Frankie: even though he has beaten her, she still loves him. Further, Frankie's questions and perspective on Jake make it clear that Jake's conclusions are unfounded. Jake was always a hothead, and Beth never wore underwear, a detail Jake uses to signify Beth's change and justify his abuse.

These details, however, make it clear that Jake has abused Beth because she will not fulfill his expectations. As Jake tells Frankie, Beth was touching herself. Jake presumes this activity indicates another, male lover. For Luce Irigaray, however, such an action is even more threatening to the masculine economy because it reminds men that women not only have sexual desire but that they also do not need a man for sexual fulfillment. Irigaray argues that "woman has sex organs more or less everywhere"; their desire is

> always something more and something else besides that *one*—sexual organ, for example—that you give them, attribute to them. Their desire is often interpreted, and feared, as a sort of insatiable hunger, a voracity that will swallow you whole. (*This Sex* 28–29)

In addition, Jake repeatedly refers to Beth's smell, and later Beth refers to it, too. This focus on feminine odor is also politically charged. As Jane Gallop argues, feminine sexuality is like feminine odor, a smell that is often condemned by the patriarchy. For Gallop such condemnation is not limited to the olfactory senses; it has political and ideological overtones. Unlike the penis, which is finite—it becomes erect, then flaccid—female odor persists. The penis may penetrate, but the feminine odor permeates. Jake's obsession with Beth's odor at this point in their relationship signifies that part of Beth, that part of women in the phallic economy, which escapes male control (*Body*).

Because of his inscription within the phallic economy, Jake cannot presume that this power belongs to Beth. There must be another man. Although he is racked with jealousy, this conclusion is much more logical than the idea of a female desire and a feminine sexuality that slips through the rigid constructions of patriarchal forms.

Beth's acting career also challenges Jake's stereotypical expectations regarding women. As Jake tells Frankie, Beth tried

to reassure him that her acting was only "pretend," but Jake
does not believe her; he knows the "truth":

> I know what they were doing! I know damn well
> what they were doin'! I know what this acting
> shit is all about. They try to "believe" they're the
> person. Right? Try to believe so hard they're the
> person that they actually think they become that
> person . . .

Frankie: What person?

Jake: The person! The—whad'ya call it? The—

Frankie: Character?

Jake: Yeah. . . . They start acting that way in real
>   life. . . . You shoulda seen the way she started to
>   walk and talk. . . . Changed her hair and every-
>   thing. Put a wig on. Changed her clothes. Every-
>   thing changed. She was unrecognizable. I didn't
>   even know who I was with anymore. . . . And
>   you know what she tells me? . . . She tells me
>   this is the real world. This acting shit is more real
>   than the real world to her. (9–10)

Jake's irritation with Beth's acting career is a gender-related
issue. As Irigaray and Lacan argue, femininity itself is a masquerade within a phallic economy. Women are constantly performing roles in order to satisfy male expectations. What disturbs Jake about Beth's acting is that he has seen the mirror
work, the machinery of femininity that he presumed unique to
him. Beth's fatal error is that she admits that the fiction is "more
real" than her life with Jake. Jake makes the connection: her role
as theatrical spectacle is more real than her life with him,
perhaps because the role the theatre provides is so explicitly
masquerade, while her life with Jake pretends to offer a real
sense of self that ultimately forces her to sacrifice her desire at
the altar of male autonomy.

Through his violent acts, Jake brutally beats Beth back into
the shape he desires. She has betrayed him through her body, so
it is her body that must be punished. Although Jake does not

articulate such motives, the play offers images in the second scene that confirm this conclusion. Beth asks her brother Mike, "Am I a mummy now?" (4). The homonym is difficult to miss. Encased in bandages, Beth is now a "mommy," physically forced into the female stereotype designed to uphold, not challenge, male expectations. For Beth, the role is a near-death experience. As she tells Mike: "I'm not dead. You go tell them. Tell them now. Go tell them. Dig me up. Tell them to dig me up now. I'm not here. They can't wait for me now" (5). To some extent, Jake has succeeded, for Beth not only persists in proclaiming her love for Jake but she also defers to Mike, using a man to articulate her desires.

Throughout the rest of the play, Beth oscillates between independence from men and dependence on them. For example, after she returns home, her mother offers her a choice between boots and slippers. Again, the image is gender-related, but Beth chooses neither "as though she does not wish to be categorized or locked into a particular sexual role" (De Rose 72). Later, moreover, she plays the man. She wears her father's shirt and nearly rapes Frankie: "You fight but all the time you want my smell. You want my shirt in your mouth. You dream of it. Always. You want me on your face" (76). Again, this masculine role is modified, for though Beth poses as a man, she refers to her feminine smell as the basis of her power. And her desire for Frankie is predicated on the fact that he change, that he become "gentle. Like a woman-man" (76). Interestingly, Frankie is symbolically castrated; his leg has been shot, so he cannot move, and therefore cannot harm Beth. He is already a "woman-man." Shepard's solution to what he calls the "terrible and impossible" relationship between the sexes ("The Silent Type" 216) appears to be some odd combination of androgyny and role reversal.

In this way, it appears that Beth offers an alternative to the usual heterosexual routine, but by the end of the play, Beth wears the trappings of all the female stereotypes: she dresses like a prostitute and behaves like an innocent virgin. The image is distressing and not entirely consistent. On the one hand, this

image could underscore the absurdity of such female stereotyping. Beth looks ridiculous in this outfit. On the other, it would
appear that despite Beth's attempts, she cannot overcome the
stereotypes. Jake has won; he has transformed her into an
object. Like the breakdown of Mary Tyrone, however, Beth's
behavior in this final scene highlights the disastrous effects of
such stereotypical roles on women. In effect, Beth has a gender-
based nervous breakdown. She becomes absolute spectacle, a
mannequin displaying all the stereotypical roles men foist upon
women.

The behavior of the lovers' family members clearly illustrates the limitations of these roles. Beth's father, Baylor, for
example, considers his mules more important than Beth's inju-
ries. He selfishly wants to keep his wife Meg and Beth separated
because he needs someone to talk to in the car. Beth characterizes him as follows: "This—this is my father. He's given up love.
Love is dead for him. My mother is dead for him. Things live for
him to be killed. Only death counts for him. Nothing else" (57).
As the play demonstrates, women, for Baylor, are only there to
serve. When they do not cooperate, Baylor disposes of them.
Beth tells Frankie that Baylor disposed of her maternal grand-
mother: "They cut her. Out. Disappeared. They don't say her
name now. She's gone. Vanish. (*She makes a "whooshing" sound
like the wind.*) My Father sent her someplace. Had her gone"
(74). When, however, Baylor needs something from the women,
the play demonstrates that he is not the independent hunter and
provider he assumes he is; he is dependent on them for both
physical and existential reassurance. Their roles and their participation are essential to male survival and identity.

Baylor's wife, Meg, submissively takes his abuse throughout much of the play. Not until the end of the play does she reach
some conclusions of her own regarding gender. When Baylor
tries to humiliate her and her mother, Meg responds that she
was not a "basket case" but instead "a female" (104). Meg's
response humanizes Baylor's objectification of her mother. More
importantly, at this point in the play, Meg begins to realize the

futility of the masculine modes of existence. The set is littered
with dead deer that no one ever eats, and it occurs to her that the
men just enjoy killing for the sake of killing. Further, the men
use hunting as an excuse to move away from love and women.
She concludes that "the female one needs the other" while the
"male goes off by himself. Leaves. He needs something else. But
he doesn't know what it is. He doesn't really know what he
needs. So he ends up dead. By himself" (105). Meg's philosophy
highlights the fact that women admit their "lack," and given a
phallic system that reminds them of it constantly, it is difficult
for them to ignore. Men, on the other hand, do not, and their
denial consequently leads to their own destruction and the
destruction of others.

Such destruction is emphasized through Sally's story of the
death of her father. Prior to this narrative, her mother, Lorraine,
has made it clear that Jake is her most important offspring. She is
completely male-identified and even tells Sally to leave her
home in order that she might have Jake all to herself. Again, the
incestuous relationship between mother and son is hinted at.
However, Jake has already won the oedipal battle, since he has
killed his father on a drinking expedition. Lorraine, however, is
ignorant of this version of the story, until Sally forces her to
listen to her interpretation of the events. In her story, the men
fiercely compete with one another, and in the end, Jake is
triumphant. This feminine narrative, however, establishes a
new and better relationship between the mother and the daughter. As a result of Sally's story, Lorraine sees the "kind of Alaska"
she has inhabited for years:

> I know one thing for sure. All these airplanes have gotta
> go. . . . All the junk in this house that they left behind for
> me to save. It's all goin'. We'll make us a big bonfire. They
> never wanted it anyway. They had no intention of ever
> comin' back here to pick it up. That was just a dream of
> theirs. It never meant a thing to them. They dreamed it all
> up just to keep me on the hook. Can't believe I fell for it all
> those years. (96)

As the earlier scenes in the play illustrate, all the men treat women like objects. Jake cannot even tell Sally from Beth and attacks her. Baylor sees all women as either burdens or mules, beasts of burden. And Mike uses Beth's illness to establish his male prowess. Lorraine realizes that she, too, was just another object, and the bonfire that she and Sally set is a symbolic gesture of independence, burning down the house that kept her captive.

For Luce Irigaray, the mother-daughter relationship is one of the most difficult to establish in a patriarchal economy. First, the psychoanalytic model of development formulated by Freud prohibits it in order to insure the daughter's proper inscription in the phallic economy and sexual marketplace. Sally and Lorraine's earlier relationship illustrates the effects of such a system: women compete with one another mercilessly in order to gain the attention of a man. Second, through the mother the daughter learns of her own castration, and she subsequently blames the mother for her "defect." Finally, the mother teaches the daughter the ways of feminine stereotypes, which result in denying the daughter's desire (*This Sex*; "One Doesn't Stir"). In this scene, however, Shepard indicates that this mother-daughter relationship, though troubled, is one of the most important in the play. Through Sally's narrative, Lorraine realizes her errors, and the two become equal adventurers in a world without their male counterparts. Though Shepard does not present any further specific images regarding this relationship, it is certainly one of the most healing and positive ones in the play.

Surprisingly, Shepard specifies the country Lorraine and Sally leave for—Ireland. While Celtic mythology provides strong female roles, as John Henry Raleigh noted in his discussion of O'Neill's *Moon for the Misbegotten*, Ireland today, particularly Catholic Ireland, maintains oppressive attitudes towards women. Even travel outside the country to obtain an abortion was considered illegal until very recently. Shepard's choice of Ireland, then, is a glaring weakness in this otherwise surprisingly liberating mother-daughter relationship.

The focus on Meg in the final scenes of the play underscores the image of hopeful and productive female relations. Meg, for example, fantasizes about a "real" wedding:

> I think it would be wonderful up on the high meadow. We could invite the whole family. We could even have a picnic up there. Cake and lemonade. We could have music. We haven't had a real wedding in so long. (114)

Meg's distinction, a "real" wedding, indicates that she envisions a different sort of relationship being established. And though her dreams for Beth and herself fulfill typical feminine roles, weddings have traditionally been the one arena in the patriarchal system over which women have had control. Later when Meg and Baylor fold the American flag together, Baylor kisses her for the first time "in twenty years." It appears that even in Meg and Baylor's home, the battle of the sexes has reached a truce.

Shepard, however, does not conclude the play on this image. Baylor proceeds upstairs alone; Jake and Mike remain outdoors playing macho, sadistic, and violent games; and Beth and Frankie's relationship is left unresolved. Meg moves away from the house to the porch, and she sees a "fire in the snow." Given the fact that Lorraine and Sally have just set fire to their "kind of Alaska," the home that imprisoned them, it is not difficult to assume that the play intends for us to make the connection. Meg, who has come to some realizations regarding her relationship with Baylor, may be on the verge of a decision that will also set fire to the "kind of Alaska" she has occupied throughout the play. Through this image, Shepard implies that the solution to both the problematic heterosexual relationships in the play and the mistreatment of women in particular is to begin anew, to destroy the old forms and start again. But like O'Neill, Shepard does not indicate whether a phoenix will rise out of the ashes of these patriarchal forms.

5

Conclusion

> I love order. It's my dream. A world where all would be
> silent and still and each thing in its last place, under the
> last dust. . . . I'm doing my best to create a little order.
>   —Clov in Beckett's *Endgame*

FEMALE characters clearly play important roles in the later
works of Eugene O'Neill, Harold Pinter, and Sam Shepard. Far
from creating stereotypical representations of women, these
three playwrights not only indict the patriarchal methods of
female objectification, but they also present female characters
who in various ways defy such methods of male objectification.

While such subtle representations certainly will not suddenly change the status of women within patriarchal culture,
they may force some audiences to reconsider their expectations
regarding femininity. In particular, an understanding of the
representations of women in these male-authored dramas may
influence subsequent theatrical productions. Since theatre, like
many institutions, has only recently begun to accept female
contributions, many biases against women remain. Furthermore, because of the spectacular nature of theatre and because
women have functioned as spectacle in patriarchal culture,
theatre may be more vulnerable to female objectification. The
process of theatrical production often imposes stereotypical
roles on the female characters in these plays, despite the plays'
attempts to avoid such modes of characterization. Geraldine
Fitzgerald's difficulties with the critics during her portrayal of
Mary Tyrone in *Long Day's Journey into Night* are a perfect
example of such misreading. Critics attacked her portrayal

because it violated their perceptions of the Madonna role. And Harold Pinter's difficulties with the Visconti production of *Old Times*, as well as the problematic critical response to Ruth in *The Homecoming*, indicate that stereotypical expectations on the part of production staff and critics can mask the subtleties and complexities of female representation in these plays.

Barbara Freedman's recent book, *Staging the Gaze*, offers an optimistic interpretation of the theatrical institution and its relationship to female representation. Rather than objectifying its content, theatre, unlike Western narrative cinema, stages the Lacanian gaze, the return of the spectator's objectifying look (1). Audiences do not merely watch a production or look at it, they are drawn in and looked at by the production. Given the recent representations of women in popular culture through music videos, advertisements, and films, representations that frequently depict women as merely body parts for male satisfaction and desire, such a conclusion is not only refreshing but it also presents theatre with an important opportunity in terms of feminism. If theatre continues to stage the gaze, rather than the look, it can become a truly effective method for feminist political change. By reminding audiences of their objectifying look, by reminding them of their stereotypical expectations, and by reminding them that their own desire influences the way they "see" not only theatre but the world, theatre can establish itself as one of the most important means for effecting political, personal, and feminist change.

Freedman, too, uses poststructuralist theory and psychoanalysis to prove her argument, and while many do not agree with all the principles set forth by this new wave of literary criticism, it has, in other genres, spawned new discussions of traditional texts. The value to such approaches, despite their attendant controversies, is that they promote rereadings of the dramatic canon that will hopefully promote the importance of theatre in Western culture, influence new productions of established texts, and spur the creation of new, contemporary works.

Freedman's book, however, uses this approach to discuss Shakespearean texts. Once again, a feminist approach to a male-authored drama occurs in the arena of Shakespearean criticism. Though feminist, poststructuralist studies that focus on the female characters in male-authored modern dramas are beginning to appear, compared to the work done in Renaissance studies, modern dramatic criticism seems cautious about offering such approaches. Most of the work in this area appears in journals and collections; few full-length studies appear. The reasons behind this situation are complex, but feminist work still needs to be done on the plays of such authors as Tennessee Williams, Samuel Beckett, Edward Albee, David Mamet, and others.

Since many of these modern playwrights consciously experiment with language, Beckett in particular, the recent discussions of gender and language by poststructuralist and psychoanalytic theorists such as Jacques Lacan, Jacques Derrida, Luce Irigaray, and Jane Gallop provide dramatic criticism with an important theoretical foundation for discussing these issues in classic texts and perhaps offer new and important readings. While many may disagree with the approaches, debates regarding the issues these theorists raise (e.g., the relationship between gender and theatrical production and between gender and language) may lead to new readings and productions of classic modern dramatic texts and may help rescue dramatic literature from its current marginalized status in the academy and in Western culture generally.

As I have witnessed through my recent work as a dramaturge and as an educational director of a regional theatre, theatre and dramatic literature, with the exception of Shakespeare, are in serious trouble. Many young people and adults have never attended a theatrical production, and most have never read dramatic literature. For whatever reason, they do not believe that theatre and drama have any place in their lives. They are not relevant, and they are not important. Even institutions that bestow grants have expressed a belief that dramatic literature is not really literature and therefore not worthy of funding. As I hope I have shown and as the few feminist, poststructuralist studies that have appeared illustrate, these theoretical principles do not cast theatre into the marginalized realm of the "cultural elite" but instead emphasize and argue for the extremely affective political, social, and cultural power of drama and theatre.[1] From a feminist perspective, approaching the works of male-authored dramas provides important insights into the nature of gender, women, and patriarchy. While some may assume that these approaches compromise feminist concerns and in effect condone misogynistic representations of women, I believe rather that such interpretations will highlight women's important role in drama specifically and in society generally. Furthermore, through discussions about the oppressive nature of patriarchy and its close relationship to culture, audiences, readers, and teachers are able to examine their own expectations of women and to account for the status of women in modern culture.

Notes
Works Cited
Index

Notes

1. Introduction

1. See, for example, Brown, Case, Chinoy and Jenkins, Dolan, Hart (*Making a Spectacle*), Keyssar, Malpede, and Wandor (*Understudies, Look Back in Gender*).

2. For a sampling of such readings on Eugene O'Neill, see Barlow, Burr, Fleche, Mandle, and Wilkins.

For readings on Harold Pinter, see Adler, Aronson, Dukore ("A Woman's Place"), Osherow, Sakellaridou, States, and Walker.

For readings on Sam Shepard, see Florence Falk, Hart ("*Fool*," "Visions"), Marranca ("Introduction"), and Watt.

3. See, for example, Freedman, Jardine, and Kahn.

4. For a fuller explanation of Lacan's complex formulations of this process, see Gallop (*Lacan*, particularly pp. 74–92).

5. The relationship between gender and language is currently the subject of much debate in the literary community. Many poststructuralist theorists argue that our language and the manner in which it functions is what they call *phallocentric*. This concept is important, and I will discuss it later, particularly in terms of the plays of Harold Pinter. For now, however, I will mention some of the theories that define phallocentrism and that influenced this project.

According to Derrida, phallocentrism is a masculine mode of discourse. It privileges closure, logic, and coherence to such an extent that it creates a linguistic prison. He attempts to show that there is "play" in this system, linguistic indeterminacy that is a creative force but that is denied expression in the phallocentric system. He often associates this play with the feminine. He discusses these issues in two important and readable essays in his collection *Writing and Difference*: "Force and Signification" (3–30) and "Structure, Sign, and Play" (278–94). For a more detailed analysis, see *Of Grammatology*. Translator Spivak's preface to this study is also enlightening.

More importantly, he argues that phallocentrism is pervasive. Athough we might realize its limits, it can never be overcome or overturned. His solution to this dilemma is as follows:

> There are thus two interpretations of interpretation, of structure, of sign, of play. The one seeks to decipher, dreams of deciphering a truth or an origin which escapes the play and the order of the sign, and which lives the necessity of interpretation as an exile. The other, which is no longer turned toward the origin, affirms play and tries to pass beyond man and humanism, the name of man being the name of that being who, throughout the history of metaphysics or of ontotheology—in other words, throughout his entire history—has dreamed of full presence, the reassuring foundation, the origin and the end of play. (*Writing and Difference* 292)

In other words, though we can never entirely escape the desire for closure, coherence, power, and logic, we must remember that these desires are illusory. Problems arise when we presume that these characteristics are attainable.

Lacan argues similarly, and his formulations regarding language, the unconscious, and gender are best presented in *Ecrits*, particularly the essay "The Agency of the Letter in the Unconscious or Reason Since Freud" (146–78). In this essay, Lacan not only sets the French linguist Ferdinand Saussure "right," but he also argues for the importance of language, the linguistic unit, in Freudian psychology, especially its effects on the formation of the human subject:

> Of course, as it is said, the letter killeth while the spirit giveth life. We can't help but agree, having had to pay homage elsewhere to a noble victim of error of seeking the spirit in the letter; but we should also like to know how the spirit could live without the letter. Even so the pretensions of the spirit would remain unassailable if the letter had not

shown us that it produces all the effects of truth in man
without involving the spirit at all. (158)

For these theorists, phallocentrism is characterized as limiting
and deadening but legislated by culture. Lacan, Derrida, and
others, however, attempt to exploit the gaps, the inconsisten-
cies, and the weaknesses of this system in order to retrieve
language's, gender's, and culture's dynamic nature.

6. For an overview of *l'écriture féminine*, see Jones.
7. See Cima, Powe, and Zinman.
8. For discussion of O'Neill's unconventional dramatic structures, see Heilman and Tornqvist. For such discussions on
Pinter, see Burkman (*Dramatic World*), Esslin (*Pinter*), Quigley
(*Pinter*), and Simard.

2. "What Is a Man Without a Good Woman's Love?": O'Neill's Madonnas

1. Almost all O'Neill studies refer to biographical material.
For a representative sampling, see the following: Bagchee,
Bloom, Bogard, Doris Falk, Manheim (*Kinship*), Raleigh ("Com-
munal"), Tiusanen, and Tornqvist. More recently, see the 1988
issue of *Theatre Annual*, the March 1988 issue of *Modern
Drama*, and *The Eugene O'Neill Newsletter* in general.

2. See Bogard (108, 301), Gelb and Gelb (8), and Sheaffer
(*Son and Artist*, particularly pp. 94–95).

3. Irigaray is not alone in this assessment. Poststructuralist
critics such as Derrida, Lacan, Gallop, and others concur. The
term *phallocentrism* focuses on the privileged status of the male
to the origin. See Derrida (*Of Grammatology*), Gallop (*Lacan*),
and Lacan (*Ecrits*).

4. While all O'Neill critics agree that the relationship
between illusion and reality is at issue in *The Iceman Cometh*,
the function of this relationship and O'Neill's opinion on this
subject are subject to debate. See, for example, Bogard, Burkman (*Godot*), Engel, Heilman, Manheim (*Kinship*), and Tornqvist.

5. Again, see the work of Derrida (*Of Grammatology*), Gallop (*Daughter's Seduction*), and Lacan (*Ecrits*).

3. "A Tick in the Night": Pinter's Whores

1. This was particularly true during the 1990 Pinter panel, "Political Pinter?," at the meeting of the Modern Language Association held in Chicago, Illinois. The debate continued during the International Harold Pinter Conference held at Ohio State University in April 1991.

2. See the following essays by Adler, Osherow, and States. See, too, the essays by Aronson, Dukore ("Woman's Place"), Sakellaridou, and Walker.

3. Esslin argues that "Pinter is not a naturalistic dramatist. This is the paradox of his artistic personality. The dialogue and the characters are real, but the over-all effect is one of mystery, of uncertainty, of poetic ambiguity" (*Pinter* 41). Katherine Burkman writes that "despite the vivid naturalism of his characters' conversations, they behave very often more like figures in a dream" (*Dramatic World* 3). Simard claims that Pinter is "neither an existentialist nor an absurdist, but a ruthless realist" (27). And Quigley argues that Pinter offers a "mixture" of "predominant conventionality" and "radical novelty" (*Pinter* 226).

4. Burkman argues that Ruth is a "savior figure" (*Godot* 126). Dukore notes that as desired object, Ruth can "turn the desirers themselves into objects manipulated by her" ("Woman's Place" 115–16). Gabbard states that "Ruth is a match for any man even Lenny" (185). And Kreps argues that "Ruth will not be bullied. . . . The victim refuses to be victimized" (30).

5. See, for example, Dukore ("Alaskan"), Esslin (*Pinter* 221–22), and Sakellaridou 204–10.

4. "Fire in the Snow": Shepard's Female Saviors

1. See, for example, Shewey's biography on Shepard, which in its subtitle describes him as a "true American original." Like

O'Neill, as well as the Eastwood character, Americans seem to grant stardom only to those writers, entertainers, etc. who, according to the American dream, create millions, texts, or music without assistance from others, yet another example of heightened self-reliance.

2. Proctor and Savran defend Shepard's early works. Auerbach ("Icarus's Mother," *Shepard*), Blau, Rabillard, Watt, and Wilson, however, view much of Shepard's work both early and present as misogynistic. Whiting has recently written an encyclopedic defense of Shepard's work ("Images").

3. See Kroll 72. See, too, Hart's comments on this relationship (*"Fool"* 215).

4. De Rose harshly accuses Shepard of pandering to his audiences: Shepard "appears to self-consciously court mainstream audiences for the first time in his career" (69).

5. Conclusion

1. Ben-Zvi, Burkman (*Godot, Dramatic World*, *"Betrayal"*), Case, Diamond, Dolan, Finney, Freedman, Hart (*Making a Spectacle*), Roof, and Schlueter all emphasize the important relationships among theory, female representation, and politics.

Works Cited

Adler, Thomas. "Notes Toward the Archetypal Pinter Woman."
  Theatre Journal 33 (1981): 377–85.

Aronson, Steven M. L. "Pinter's 'Family' and Blood Knowledge." Lahr 67–86.

Auerbach, Doris. *Sam Shepard, Arthur Kopit, and Off-Broad-
  way Theater.* Boston: Twayne, 1982.

———. "Who Was Icarus's Mother? The Powerless Mother
  Figures in the Plays of Sam Shepard." King 53–64.

Bagchee, Shyamal, ed. *Perspectives on O'Neill: New Essays.*
  Victoria: U of Victoria P, 1988.

Barlow, Judith. "O'Neill's Many Mothers: Mary Tyrone, Josie
  Hogan, and Their Antecedents." Bagchee 7–17.

Ben-Zvi, Linda. "Harold Pinter's *Betrayal*: The Patterns of
  Banality." *Modern Drama* 23 (1980): 227–37.

———, ed. *Women in Beckett: Performance and Critical Studies.* Urbana: U of Illinois P, 1990.

Bernheimer, Charles. "Introduction: Part One." In *Dora's Case:
  Freud, Hysteria, and Feminism.* Ed. Charles Bernheimer
  and Claire Kahane. New York: Columbia UP, 1985. 1–18.

Bettelheim, Bruno. *The Uses of Enchantment: The Meaning and
  Importance of Fairy Tales.* New York: Vintage, 1976.

Bigsby, C. W. E. *A Critical Introduction to Twentieth-Century
  American Drama: Beyond Broadway.* Vol. 3. New York:
  Cambridge UP, 1985.

Black, Stephen. "Letting the Dead be Dead: A Reinterpretation
  of *A Moon for the Misbegotten.*" *Modern Drama* 29 (1986):
  544–55.

Blau, Herbert. "The American Dream in American Gothic: The
  Plays of Sam Shepard and Adrienne Kennedy." *Modern
  Drama* 27 (1984): 520–39.

Bloom, Harold, ed. "Introduction." *Eugene O'Neill's "Long*

Day's Journey into Night." New York: Chelsea House, 1987. 1–8.

Bogard, Travis. *Contour in Time: The Plays of Eugene O'Neill.* Rev. ed. New York: Oxford UP, 1988.

Braidotti, Rose. "The Politics of Ontological Difference." *Between Feminism and Psychoanalysis.* Ed. Teresa Brennan. New York: Routledge, 1989. 89–105.

Brater, Enoch. "Cinematic Fidelity and the Forms of Harold Pinter's *Betrayal.*" *Modern Drama* 24 (1981): 503–13.

Brecht, Bertolt. *Brecht on Theatre.* Trans. John Willett. New York: Hill and Wang, 1964.

Brown, Janet. *Feminist Drama: Definition and Critical Analysis.* Metuchen, NJ: Scarecrow Press, 1979.

Brustein, Robert. *The Theater of Revolt.* Boston: Little, 1964.

Burkman, Katherine. *The Arrival of Godot: Ritual Patterns in Modern Drama.* Rutherford: Farleigh Dickinson UP, 1986.

———. *The Dramatic World of Harold Pinter: Its Basis in Ritual.* Columbus: Ohio State University Press, 1971.

———. "Harold Pinter's *Betrayal*: Life Before Death and After." *Theatre Journal* 34 (1982): 505–18.

Burr, Suzanne. "O'Neill's Ghostly Women." Schlueter 37–47.

Butler, Judith. *Gender Trouble: Feminism and the Subversion of Identity.* New York: Routledge, 1990.

Case, Sue-Ellen. *Feminism and Theatre.* New York: Methuen, 1988.

Chinoy, Helen Krich, and Linda Walsh Jenkins. *Women in American Theatre.* Rev. and expanded. New York: Theatre Communications Group, 1987.

Chothia, Jean. *Forging a Language: A Study of the Plays of Eugene O'Neill.* Cambridge: Cambridge UP, 1979.

Cima, Gay Gibson. "Shifting Perspectives: Combining Shepard and Rauschenberg." *Theatre Journal* 38 (1986): 67–81.

Cixous, Hélène. "Aller a la mer." Trans. Barbara Kerslake. *Modern Drama* 27 (1984): 546–48.

———. "Castration or Decapitation." Trans. Annette Kuhn. *Signs* 7.1 (1981): 41–55.

De Rose, David. "Slouching Towards Broadway: Shepard's *A Lie of the Mind.*" *Theatre* 17 (1986): 69–74.

Derrida, Jacques. *Of Grammatology.* Trans. Gayatri Chakravorty Spivak. Baltimore: Johns Hopkins UP, 1976.

———. *Writing and Difference.* Ed. and Trans. Alan Bass. Chicago: U of Chicago P, 1978.

Diamond, Elin. *Pinter's Comic Play.* Lewisburg: Bucknell UP, 1985.

Dolan, Jill. *The Feminist Spectator as Critic.* Ann Arbor: UMI Research P, 1988.

Dukore, Bernard. "Alaskan Perspectives." *Harold Pinter: You Never Heard Such Silence.* Ed. Alan Bold. New York: Barnes, 1984. 166–77.

———. "A Woman's Place." Lahr 109–16.

Engel, Edwin A. *The Haunted Heroes of Eugene O'Neill.* Cambridge: Harvard UP, 1953.

Engels, Frederick. *The Origin of the Family, Private Property, and The State.* Ed. Eleanor Burke Leacock. New York: International, 1973.

Esslin, Martin. *Pinter: The Playwright.* Rev. ed. New York: Methuen, 1984.

———. *The Theatre of the Absurd.* Rev. ed. New York: Overlook, 1973.

Falk, Doris. *Eugene O'Neill and the Tragic Tension: An Interpretive Study of the Plays.* New Brunswick, NJ: Rugers UP, 1958.

Falk, Florence. "Men Without Women: The Shepard Landscape." Marranca 90–103.

Felski, Rita. *Beyond Feminist Aesthetics: Feminist Literature and Social Change.* Cambridge: Harvard UP, 1989.

Fetterley, Judith. *The Resisting Reader: A Feminist Approach to American Fiction.* Bloomington: Indiana UP, 1978.

Finney, Gail. *Women in Modern Drama: Freud, Feminism, and European Theater at the Turn of the Century.* Ithaca: Cornell UP, 1989.

Fitzgerald, Geraldine. "Another Neurotic Electra." Floyd 290–92.

Fjelde, Rolf. "Plotting Pinter's Progress." Lahr 87–108.

Fleche, Anne. "A Monster of Perfection: O'Neill's 'Stella'." Schlueter 25–36.

Floyd, Virginia, ed. *Eugene O'Neill: A World View*. New York: Ungar, 1979.

Freedman, Barbara. *Staging the Gaze: Postmodern, Psychoanalysis, and Shakespearean Comedy*. Ithaca: Cornell UP, 1991.

Freud, Sigmund. "Some Psychological Consequences of the Anatomical Distinctions Between the Sexes." *Sexuality and the Psychology of Love*. Ed. Philip Rieff. New York: Collier, 1963. 183–93.

Friedan, Betty. *The Feminine Mystique*. New York: Dell, 1974.

Gabbard, Lucinda P. *The Dream Structure of Pinter's Plays: A Psychoanalytic Approach*. Rutherford: Farleigh Dickinson UP, 1976.

Gale, Stephen. *Butter's Going Up: A Critical Analysis of Harold Pinter's Work*. Durham: Duke UP, 1977.

Gallop, Jane. *The Daughter's Seduction: Feminism and Psychoanalysis*. Ithaca: Cornell UP, 1982.

————. *Reading Lacan*. Ithaca: Cornell UP, 1985.

————. *Thinking Through the Body*. New York: Columbia UP, 1988.

Ganz, Arthur. "Mixing Memory and Desire: Pinter's Vision in *Landscape*, *Silence*, and *Old Times*." Ganz 161–78.

————, ed. *Pinter: A Collection of Critical Essays*. Englewood Cliffs, NJ: Prentice, 1972.

Gelb, Arthur, and Barbara Gelb. *O'Neill*. New York: Harper, 1962.

Gledhill, Christine. "The Melodramatic Field: An Investigation." *Home Is Where the Heart Is: Studies in Melodrama and the Women's Film*. Ed. Christine Gledhill. London: British Film Institute, 1987. 5–43.

Grimm, Jacob, and Wilhelm Grimm. "Brier Rose (Sleeping Beauty)." *The Complete Fairy Tales of the Brothers Grimm*. Trans. Jack Zipes. New York: Bantam, 1987. 186–89.

Grosz, Elizabeth. *Jacques Lacan: A Feminist Introduction*. New York: Routledge, 1990.

Gussow, Mel. "Pinter's Plays Follow Him Into Politics." *New York Times* 6 Dec. 1988, late ed.: 17+.

Hall, Peter. "A Director's Approach: An Interview with Peter Hall." Lahr 9–26.

Halton, Kathleen. "Pinter." *Vogue* Oct. 1967: 194–95.

Hart, Lynda. Ed. *Making a Spectacle: Feminist Essays on Contemporary Women's Theatre*. Ann Arbor: U of Michigan P, 1989.

———. *Sam Shepard's Metaphorical Stages*. Westport, CT: Greenwood, 1987.

———. "Sam Shepard's Pornographic Visions." *Studies in the Literary Imagination* 21.2 (1988): 69–82.

———. "Sam Shepard's Spectacle of Impossible Heterosexuality: *Fool for Love*." Schlueter 213–26.

Heilman, Robert. *The Iceman, the Arsonist and the Troubled Agent: Tragedy and Melodrama on the Modern Stage*. Seattle: U of Washington P, 1973.

Heller, Adele, and Lois Rudnick. "Introduction." *1915: The Cultural Moment: The New Politics, the New Woman, the New Psychology, the New Art, and the New Theatre in America*. New Brunswick, NJ: Rutgers UP, 1991. 1–14.

Hewes, Henry. "Probing Pinter's Play." *Saturday Review* 8 Apr. 1967: 56.

Hinden, Michael. "Desire and Forgiveness: O'Neill's Diptych." *Comparative Drama* 14 (1980): 240–50.

Hunter, Dianne. "Hysteria, Psychoanalysis, and Feminism." *The M(Other) Tongue: Essays in Feminist Psychoanlytic Interpretation*. Ed. Shirley Nelson Garner, Claire Kahane, and Madelon Sprengnether. Ithaca: Cornell UP, 1985. 89–118.

Irigaray, Luce. "And One Doesn't Stir Without the Other." Trans. Hélène Vivienne Wenzel. *Signs* 7.1 (1981): 60–67.

———. *Speculum of the Other Woman*. Trans. Gillian C. Gill. Ithaca: Cornell UP, 1985.

————. *This Sex Which Is Not One.* Trans. Catherine Porter. Ithaca: Cornell UP, 1985.

Jardine, Lisa. *Still Harping on Our Daughters: Women and Drama in the Age of Shakespeare.* 2nd ed. New York: Columbia UP, 1989.

Jones, Ann Rosalind. "Writing the Body: Toward an Understanding of *l'Écriture féminine.*" Showalter 361–78.

Kahn, Coppelia. "The Absent Mother in *King Lear.*" *Rewriting the Renaissance: The Discourse of Sexual Difference in Early Modern Europe.* Ed. Margaret Ferguson et al. Chicago: U of Chicago P, 1986. 33–49.

Kaplan, Louise. *Female Perversions: The Temptations of Emma Bovary.* New York: Doubleday, 1991.

Kennedy, Douglas. "Breaking the Silence." *New Statesman and Society* 28 Oct. 1988: 38–39.

Keyssar, Helene. *Feminist Theatre.* New York: Grove, 1985.

King, Kimball, ed. *Sam Shepard: A Casebook.* New York: Garland, 1988.

Kleb, William. "Worse Than Being Homeless: True West and the Divided Self." Marranca 117–25.

Klein, Ethel. *Gender Politics: From Consciousness to Mass Politics.* Cambridge: Harvard UP, 1984.

Kolodny, Annette. "Dancing Through the Minefield." Showalter 144–67.

————. *The Land Before Her: Fantasy and Experience of the American Frontiers, 1630–1860.* Chapel Hill: U of North Carolina P, 1984.

Kreps, Barbara. "Time and Harold Pinter's Possible Realities: Art as Life, and Vice Versa." *Modern Drama* 22 (1979): 47–60.

Kroll, Jack. With Constance Gutherie and Janet Huck. "Who's That Tall Dark Stranger?" *Newsweek* 11 Nov. 1985: 68–72.

Lacan, Jacques. *Ecrits: A Selection.* Trans. Alan Sheridan. New York: Norton, 1977.

————. *Feminine Sexuality.* Ed. Juliet Mitchell and Jacqueline Rose. Trans. Jacqueline Rose. New York: Norton, 1982.

Lahr, John, ed. *A Casebook on Harold Pinter's "The Homecoming."* New York: Grove, 1971.

Lévi-Strauss, Claude. *The Elementary Structures of Kinship.* Trans. James Harle Bell et al. Rev. ed. Boston: Beacon, 1969.

Londré, Felicia Hardison. "Sam Shepard Works Out: The Masculinization of America." *Studies in American Drama: 1945–Present* 2 (1987): 19–27.

Malpede, Karen. *Women in Theatre: Compassion and Hope.* New York: Drama Book Specialists, 1983.

Mandl, Bette. "Theatricality and Otherness in *All God's Children Got Wings.*" Schlueter 48–56.

Manheim, Michael. *Eugene O'Neill's New Language of Kinship.* Syracuse: Syracuse UP, 1982.

———. "O'Neill's Transcendence of Melodrama in *A Touch of the Poet* and *A Moon for the Misbegotten.*" *Critical Approaches to O'Neill.* Ed. John Stroupe. New York: AMS Press, 1988: 147–59.

Marranca, Bonnie, ed. *American Dreams: The Imagination of Sam Shepard.* New York: PAJ, 1981.

———. "Introduction." Marranca 13–36.

———. "Sam Shepard." *American Playwrights: A Critical Survey.* Vol. 1. Ed. Bonnie Marranca and Gautam Dasgupta. New York: Drama Book Specialists, 1981. 81–111.

Merritt, Susan Hollis. *Pinter in Play: Critical Strategies and the Plays of Harold Pinter.* Durham: Duke UP, 1990.

Mitchell, Juliet. *Psychoanalysis and Feminism: Freud, Reich, Laing, and Women.* New York: Vintage, 1975.

Modleski, Tania. *Loving with a Vengeance: Mass-Produced Fantasies for Women.* New York: Routledge, 1990.

Mulvey, Laura. *Visual and Other Pleasures.* Bloomington: Indiana UP, 1989.

O'Neill, Eugene. *Eugene O'Neill: The Complete Plays: 1932–1943.* Vol. 3. Ed. Travis Bogard. New York: Library of America, 1988.

———. *The Iceman Cometh. Complete Plays.* 561–712.

————. *Long Day's Journey into Night. Complete Plays.* 713–828.

————. *A Moon for the Misbegotten. Complete Plays.* 853–946.

————. *Selected Letters of Eugene O'Neill.* Ed. Travis Bogard and Jackson Byer. New Haven: Yale UP, 1988.

Osherow, Anita R. "Mother and Whore: The Role of Woman in *The Homecoming.*" *Modern Drama* 17 (1974): 423–32.

Pinter, Harold. *Betrayal. The Complete Works: Four.* New York: Grove, 1981. 155–268.

————. "Harold Pinter: An Interview." By Lawrence Bensky. Ganz 19–33.

————. *The Homecoming.* New York: Grove, 1966.

————. *No Man's Land. The Complete Works: Four.* New York: Grove, 1981. 73–154.

————. *Other Places: A Kind of Alaska, Victoria Station, Family Voices.* New York: Grove, 1983.

————. "A Play and Its Politics. A Conversation Between Harold Pinter and Nicholas Hern." *One for the Road.* New York: Grove, 1984. 5–23.

————. "Postscript." *One for the Road.* New York: Grove, 1984. 24.

Postlewait, Thomas. "Pinter's *The Homecoming*: Displacing and Repeating Ibsen." *Comparative Drama* 15 (1981): 195–212.

Powe, Bruce. "*The Tooth of Crime*: Sam Shepard's Way with Music." *Modern Drama* 24 (1981): 13–25.

Proctor, Elizabeth. "Offbeat Humor and Comic Mystery in Shepard's Plays: *La Turista, The Unseen Hand, The Mad Dog Blues*, and *Forensic and the Navigators.*" King 31–51.

Quigley, Austin. *The Modern Stage and Other Worlds.* New York: Methuen, 1985.

————. *The Pinter Problem.* Princeton: Princeton UP, 1975.

Rabillard, Sheila. "Sam Shepard: Theatrical Power and American Drama." *Modern Drama* 30 (1987): 58–71.

Rahill, Frank. *The World of Melodrama.* University Park: Penn State UP, 1967.

Raleigh, John Henry. "Communal, Familial, and Personal Memories in O'Neill's *Long Day's Journey into Night*." *Modern Drama* 31 (1988): 63–72.

———. "The Irish Atavism of *A Moon for the Misbegotten*." Floyd 229–36.

Robinson, James. "The Metatheatrics of *A Moon for the Misbegotten*." Bagchee 61–75.

Roof, Judith. "Marguerite Duras and the Question of a Feminist Theatre." *Feminism and Psychoanalysis*. Ed. Richard Feldstein and Judith Roof. Ithaca: Cornell, UP, 1989. 323–40.

Rose, Jacqueline. Introduction: II. Lacan, *Feminine Sexuality*. 27–58.

Sacks, Oliver. *Awakenings*. Rev. ed. New York: Dutton, 1983.

Sakellaridou, Elizabeth. *Pinter's Female Portraits: A Study of Female Characters in the Plays of Harold Pinter*. London: MacMillan, 1988.

Sarbin, Deborah. "'I Decided She Was': Representation of Women in *The Homecoming*." *The Pinter Review: Annual Essays 1989*. 34–42.

Savran, David. "Sam Shepard's Conceptual Prison: *Action* and *The Unseen Hand*." *Theatre Journal* 36 (1984): 57–73.

Schiff, Stephen. "Pinter's Passions." *Vanity Fair* Sept. 1990: 219–303.

Schlueter, June, ed. *Feminist Rereadings of Modern American Drama*. Rutherford: Farleigh Dickinson UP, 1989.

Sheaffer, Louis. *O'Neill: Son and Artist*. New York: Little, 1973.

———. *O'Neill: Son and Playwright*. New York: Little, 1968.

Shepard, Sam. *Buried Child*. *Seven Plays*. New York: Bantam, 1981. 61–132.

———. Interview. "Myths, Dreams, Realities—Sam Shepard's America." By Michiko Kakutani. *New York Times* 29 Jan. 1984, late ed., sec. 2: 1+.

———. Interview. "The Silent Type." By Stephen Fay. *Vogue* Feb. 1985:213–18.

———. *A Lie of the Mind*. New York: NAL, 1986.

———. *Paris, Texas*. Ed. Chris Sievernich. Adapted by L. M. Kit Carson. Berlin: Road Movies, 1984.

————. *True West*. *Seven Plays*. New York: Bantam, 1981. 1–59.

————. "The *True West* Interviews." By John Dark. *West Coast Plays* 9 (1981): 51–71.

Shewey, Don. *Sam Shepard: The Life, the Loves, Behind the Legend of a True American Original*. New York: Dell, 1985.

Showalter, Elaine, ed. *The New Feminist Criticism: Essays on Women, Literature, and Theory*. New York: Pantheon, 1985.

Silverman, Kaja. *The Subject of Semiotics*. New York: Oxford UP, 1983.

Simard, Rodney. *Postmodern Drama: Contemporary Playwrights in America and Britain*. Lanham: UP of America, 1984.

Spivak, Gayatri Chakravorty. Preface. Derrida, *Of Grammatology*. ix–lxxxvii.

States, Bert O. "Pinter's *The Homecoming*: The Shock of Non-recognition." Ganz 147–60.

Storch, R. F. "Harold Pinter's Happy Families." Ganz. 136–46.

Taylor, John Russell. "Pinter's Game of Happy Families." Lahr 57–66.

Tiusanen, Timo. *O'Neill's Scenic Images*. Princeton: Princeton UP, 1968.

Tornqvist, Egil. *A Drama of Souls: Studies in O'Neill's Super-Naturalistic Technique*. New Haven: Yale UP, 1969.

Trussler, Simon. *The Plays of Harold Pinter: An Assessment*. London: Gollancz, 1973.

Van Laan, Thomas F. "*The Dumb Waiter*: Pinter's Play with the Audience." *Modern Drama* 24 (1981): 494–502.

Varley, Alan. "Actor, Author, and Audience: Scene 7 of Harold Pinter's *Betrayal*." *Cycnos* 3 (1986–87): 95–109.

Walker, Augusta. "Why the Lady Does It." Lahr 117–22.

Wandersee, Winifred. *On the Move: American Women in the 1970's*. Boston: Twayne, 1988.

Wandor, Michelene. *Carry On, Understudies: Theatre and Sexual Politics*. New York: Routledge, 1986.

————. *Look Back in Gender: Sexuality and the Family in Post-War British Drama*. New York: Methuen, 1987.

Watt, Stephen. "Simulation, Gender, and Postmodernism: Sam Shepard and *Paris, Texas*." *Perspectives on Contemporary Literature* 13 (1987): 73–82.

Whiting, Charles G. "Digging Up *Buried Child*." *Modern Drama* 31 (1988): 548–56.

――――. "Images of Women in Shepard's Theatre." *Modern Drama* 33 (1990): 494–506.

Wilkins, Fredrick, ed. *O'Neill's Women*. Special issue of *The Eugene O'Neill Newsletter*. 6.2 (1982).

Williams, Raymond. *Drama from Ibsen to Brecht*. London: Hogarth, 1987.

Wilson, Ann. "The Fool of Desire: The Spectator to the Plays of Sam Shepard." *Modern Drama* 30 (1987): 46–57.

Wimsatt, W. K. *The Verbal Icon: Studies in the Meaning of Poetry*. Lexington: U of Kentucky P, 1954.

Woodruff, Robert. "Interview with Robert Woodruff." By Robert Coe. Marranca 151–158.

Woolf, Virginia. *A Room of One's Own*. New York: Harcourt, 1929.

Zinman, Toby Silverman. "Sam Shepard and Super-Realism." *Modern Drama* 29 (1986): 423–30.

Index

Ann C. Hall received her Ph.D. from Ohio State University. As an assistant professor of English at Marquette University, she taught courses on drama and playwriting before becoming the Education Director and Dramaturge for The Contemporary American Theatre Company in Columbus, Ohio, where she teaches playwriting and works with local arts councils, high schools, colleges, and universities. She is also the treasurer for the Harold Pinter Society.

She has written articles on Eugene O'Neill, Harold Pinter, Sam Shepard, and David Mamet. Several of her original plays have been published and produced. She is currently at work on two scholarly projects: "Wimps, Weasels, and Whiners: Men in Twentieth-Century Fiction" and "Pathological Independence: The Life and Work of Maria Irene Fornes."